WHO'S GOT THE POWER?

Also by Dave Kamper

Double Steal: A Danny and Carol Alexander Mystery

WHO'S GOT THE POWER?

The Resurgence of American Unions

DAVE KAMPER

THE
NEW
PRESS

NEW YORK
LONDON

Requests for permission to reproduce selections from this book should be made through our website: https://thenewpress.org/contact-us.

Published in the United States by The New Press, New York, 2025

Distributed by Two Rivers Distribution

ISBN 978-1-62097-908-2 (hc)
ISBN 978-1-62097-995-2 (ebook)
CIP data is available

The New Press publishes books that promote and enrich public discussion and understanding of the issues vital to our democracy and to a more equitable world. These books are made possible by the enthusiasm of our readers; the support of a committed group of donors, large and small; the collaboration of our many partners in the independent media and the not-for-profit sector; booksellers, who often hand-sell New Press books; librarians; and above all by our authors.

www.thenewpress.org

Composition by Dix Digital Prepress and Design
This book was set in Adobe Garamond and Janson Text

Printed in the United States of America

10 9 8 7 6 5 4 3 2 1

Contents

Foreword

On February 8, 2025, I stood on the tarmac at Washington National Airport to say goodbye to Danasia Elder. As I watched the plane that carried her body depart for her final flight, one of Danasia's colleagues turned to me, and said, "Now I really understand why we need a union."

Just after 9 p.m. on January 29, 2025, I got the call that PSA Airlines / American Eagle Flight 5342 had been involved in a midair crash on approach to Washington National Airport with two of our members working in the cabin.

Our union, the Association of Flight Attendants, immediately mobilized. Our Employee Assistance Program critical incident response moved quickly to ensure every flight attendant working received positive contact and had access to trauma response, with a support hotline available 24/7 to all flight attendants at PSA and across the industry. We made sure that flight attendants who were deeply affected by the crash could trade trips and call off without disciplinary action. We dedicated donations to our disaster relief fund to the families of Danasia Elder and Ian Epstein, the two AFA crewmembers working the flight.

We also took up our role in aviation safety. Two AFA-CWA members—flight attendants who specifically trained for the job as part of our union's health and safety team—rushed to arrive on the scene to serve on the National Transportation Safety Board's accident investigation team. Once union first responders and recovery teams had recovered the bodies, we worked to make sure Danasia and Ian returned home with dignity and honor.

So when the AFA member said to me, as we stood together to honor Danasia's last flight, "Now I really understand why we need a union," it both warmed and broke my heart.

Far too many American workers—union and non-union—don't realize what a union is for until they need one. And when you realize you need a union, it's usually too late. Solidarity is a force stronger than gravity. It can be used at all times to protect and advance the interests of workers if we dare to raise expectations through knowledge of our collective strength.

This book tells working-class stories. Some of the workers you'll learn about realized that they needed a union. Some of the workers realized their union could only deliver what they were willing to fight for. And some fought for and won things that no one thought possible.

As I write this in February 2025, our working class is under attack and our democracy is on the verge of collapse due to massive inequality. Reliance on "legal protections" may prove entirely foolish, but the hope of solidarity coupled with a clear worker agenda may be our only chance to stop oppressive, authoritarian rule in order to save our planet and our basic human rights.

On the one hand, the workers you'll read about in this book—and millions like them—are rising up. More Americans approve of unions and want to belong to one than at any point since before I was born. Young people are fed up with the lie that we should live to work. Older workers are realizing that they were sold a lie when the boss said, "Keep your head down, do a good job, and it'll all be taken care of."

On the other hand, we're in real trouble. According to the latest data from the Bureau of Labor Statistics, only 9.9 percent of American workers belonged to a union in 2024. In the private sector, where unions are the only effective check on the unbridled greed of robber barons like Elon Musk, that number is just 5.9 percent.

This historic gap couldn't come at a worse time. The corporate elite have been working methodically for eighty years to overturn the social agreement working people forged through solidarity and sacrifice as we rose out of the Great Depression.

They are on the verge of fully realizing their goals.

In 2024, a handful of billionaires spent hundreds of millions of dollars each to buy America's elections. Now, they're using the power they bought to drive what they mean to be the final nail in our collective coffin.

Elon Musk—perhaps the world's loudest and proudest union buster—is smashing our democracy with a sledgehammer. He's working to force out dedicated federal workers and cut off the life-saving work they do. He's destroying agencies and departments that are very much like our unions. You don't realize you need them until you do, and then it just might be too late.

As a flight attendant, I know my safety relies on those workers every time I step on a plane. The safety measures that make accidents like Flight 5342 so rare didn't always exist—and many of them wouldn't exist without the work of aviation unions.

I could have easily been on board United Flight 175 on September 11, 2001. But instead it was my friends and flying partners Amy, Al, Kathryn, Alicia, Amy, Michael, and Robert who died when hijackers flew the plane into the South Tower of the World Trade Center.

While first responders, including thousands of federal workers, were still searching for bodies and clearing rubble, our union was fighting to establish the Transportation Security Administration. We worked to create a national standard for airport security—and to make sure the TSA would serve as a central hub behind the scenes for every agency to share intelligence about aviation security.

I know that the planes I board are safe because of tens of thousands of federal workers at more than a dozen agencies who inspect our planes, protect our airports, and watch our skies. I also know that many of their jobs exist because nearly a million aviation workers come together through our unions and demand safe workplaces.

The regulations federal workers enforce—the ones we helped write—have been the first target for Musk and his operation. The billionaires hate "regulation" because it's a check on their power and their profits. As they work to smash the agencies that keep us all safe, they're operating straight out of the playbook they use to destroy workplace solidarity.

The union buster's playbook has four D's—divide, distract, delay, demoralize. This book tells the stories of workers who overcame those tactics. Baristas who refused to be divided when Starbucks (illegally) dangled new benefits in front of them, but only for non-union stores—and instead built an organizing juggernaut. Actors and writers who found new strength and solidarity as studio bosses worked to distract them with a blizzard of disinformation fed through industry-friendly press—and emerged with a historic contract. Grad students who refused to let Dartmouth delay certification of their union by challenging hundreds of votes—and instead organized a counterstrategy that toppled the boss's plan. Flight attendants who refused to be demoralized when all the "experts" told us there was no way we could get Congress to guarantee our paychecks—and instead pushed forward to secure an historic worker-first package that saved our entire industry from ruin.

When I first spoke with Dave about writing this foreword, I was struck by something he said. He told me this was "an optimistic book for a perilous time." That was before the 2024 election results came in, and the times are even more perilous now.

I asked how I could contribute. He wanted me to write about what I've seen over three decades in the labor movement, and most importantly what I see coming next.

Some of that may be much clearer by the time you're reading this. From where I stand now, it's hard to see through the furious assault on our future. I have no illusions about how difficult the coming years will be. But I hope—and I know—that if we deny them the four D's and instead practice solidarity we will win.

The danger we face is unlike any Americans have faced in living memory. These billionaire robber barons are laying dynamite at the very foundations of our democracy. They've whittled our labor movement down to almost nothing. They're gunning for our civil rights and our human rights. They are spreading a message of scarcity to encourage fighting among the working class.

They are running the union buster's playbook, and at first glance it's working like a charm. It's hard to imagine a country more divided and distracted, or an opposition more demoralized.

But that playbook is tired. The people in this book found new ways to beat it. And I have also seen time and again that solidarity is most often born from necessity.

When the pandemic hit, aviation unions were at each other's throats as often as we had one another's backs. The bosses had spent years driving wedges between pilots and flight attendants, onboard crews and ground crews, even between one flight attendant union and another.

But when our entire industry faced collapse, we found a new kind of solidarity. After we saved our industry (you'll read about that later), the companies tried to put the screws to us in our contracts. That fight is still raging, but we have shown up for each other in ways we had never done before. For the first time since I signed a union card twenty-nine years ago, it doesn't matter what job you do, the color of the uniform, or the logo on the tail of the plane. In a way that's new to our industry, we mean it when we say we're all in it together.

It will take radical solidarity to save our union movement. And I believe a thriving, fighting union movement is the only thing that can save our country and our world.

The billionaires and their shills know that, and it's why the union movement has been at the top target on their list since the first workers linked arms. Our social contract was built by everyday people coming together in our workplaces and demanding more for everyone. When my dad was entering the workforce, one in three workers had a union contract. Working people could wield tremendous power in our workplaces and in government. But they've worked steadily for eighty years since the Taft–Hartley Act was passed in 1947, which curtailed the power of unions, and now they think that our working-class movement is on its deathbed.

Here's a piece of inspiration I offer you. Today's corporate elite—all waving their MBAs and toasting each other with golden goblets—have forgotten that a fair shake is the price they agreed to pay for peaceful labor. And the politicians they bought have forgotten that a functioning government and a working democracy is the price they pay for a stable nation. They've made no secret that they plan to destroy the rules that give working people any chance to thrive. But once they destroy the rules, it's up to us to remind them that the rules and the agreements we made were the only thing holding us in check, too.

When West Virginia teachers marched on the state capitol, they had no right to strike. They had no bargaining power at the legislature. But every one of us has the power to withhold our labor—we just have to find the will to link arms and do it.

In 2019, as the federal shutdown entered its seventh week, I stood alongside both federal-sector and private-sector workers. We warned the country that our system was stretched to the breaking point. Hours later, air traffic at LaGuardia stopped when air traffic controllers called out from exhaustion and the airport couldn't staff the tower.

The longest shutdown in our history ended within hours. But here's the real secret. They ended the shutdown because they didn't want the rest of us to realize that we have the power to grind this whole thing to a dead stop. They are afraid that we'll realize that we are the ones with the power.

The union busters are afraid of us. It may seem like we're hopelessly divided right now. But the workers who launched the strike that in 2023 brought the Big Three to the table—and delivered historic contracts—don't share political beliefs. They come from every background you can imagine. Native-born and immigrant. Black and white. Straight and queer. Cisgender and trans. When the boss took it one step too far, they showed the whole world who really held the cards.

I hope—I believe—that the working class can find that same solidarity. It's up to each one of us to help find it.

On April 3, 1968, Dr. Martin Luther King Jr. stood in front of striking sanitation workers in Memphis, Tennessee. He told them, "I've seen the Promised Land. I may not get there with you. But I want you to know tonight, that we, as a people, will get to the promised land!"

I believe Dr. King meant that none of us is individually responsible for leading our country and our world to a better future—but we are all collectively responsible to each other. We either get there together, or we perish in the desert. Dr. King was gunned down the next day, but he left the charge with all of us to carry each other forward as far as we can.

There is another line from that speech that I love. It's something I try to remember in moments when I want to give up. He said, "Whenever men and women straighten their backs up, they are going somewhere, because a man can't ride your back unless it is bent."

The next few years will be a perilous time. And every great people's movement in history sprang from perilous times. Moments when a wealthy few got so greedy that there was nothing left for the rest of us. Moments when the powerful got so arrogant that they never saw us coming. As I write this, I know that things are going to get bad. Working people have a choice. We can bend our backs. We can duck our heads and hide (some of us, quite literally, may have to hide in basements and attics). Or we can link arms and fight.

It's time for us to break free of the conventions and assumptions that divide us—like the idea that somehow there's a difference between the poor, the working class, and the middle class. It's time to realize there are the billionaires and there's everyone else. Then it's time to straighten our backs, link our arms, and get to work.

The only way to that promised land is together. Let's decide that we're willing to fight for the chance for our kids or their kids to get there, even if we never make it ourselves.

I hope this book will inspire you like it inspired me. I hope that in these stories you'll find a new idea, a new strategy, a new motivation to link arms with someone you don't know. I hope you'll find the courage to look someone who seems to have nothing in common with you in the eye and say, "I've got your back."

Sara Nelson
International President
Association of Flight Attendants-CWA, AFL-CIO
February 2025

WHO'S GOT THE POWER?

Introduction

In the small gaps of time between customers, Starbucks baristas talk quietly to each other about the disrespect the company shows them.

As they peel off their hazmat suits after cleaning the production line in Topeka, the people who make our Cheetos resolve to stick together and walk out.

Victims of sexual violence on campus, faced with a university that values the reputation of its star faculty more than the health and safety of everyone else, find a space to share their anger and find allies.

Workaday Hollywood actors, the ones whose names we don't know, borrow money from each other to pay the rent as millions of us watch them on Netflix, and decide to do something about it.

Middle-aged autoworkers, living out of a long-stay hotel as they are shuffled from one closing plant to another, bring in militant new leaders for their union and launch the most important strike in the twenty-first century.

The first half of the 2020s has seen the biggest union upsurge in perhaps fifty years. In every kind of workplace, every kind of industry, in every corner of the country, we've seen organizing drives, contract fights, innovative tactics, and strikes coming at an intensity we're just not used to anymore.

We used to be used to it. There was a time when unions were a central player in every aspect of American life. Union leaders like John L. Lewis, George Meany, and Walter Reuther were feted by presidents of both parties, and, when they gave speeches, they could count on the front pages of every major newspaper in the country to carry them. Wage increases which unions won at the bargaining table set the standard for workers across the country. Every decent-sized town had one or more union halls, and those halls were beehives of activity year-round. One in every three workers had a union, and half of Americans lived in a union household. Unions printed their contracts small enough that they could fit in your front shirt pocket, so you could whip it out and cite chapter and verse to show up a lousy supervisor, with the knowledge that the largest civic institution the nation (the world) had ever seen—the American labor movement—would have your back.

Not so much anymore.

Now, barely one in sixteen private-sector workers is a member of a union. Whole swaths of the country are organized-labor deserts, even for the comparatively better-off public-sector unions.* Union leaders, with just a handful of exceptions, are barely known outside (or, let's be honest, often inside) the movement. One of the nation's major political parties largely takes labor unions for granted, and the other feels free to openly wage war upon them, knowing unions are often too weak to fight back.

I've been a part of this movement for more than twenty-five years. In that time, unions have shrunk by about 2 million members even though there are 25 million more people employed. I'd

---

* This book can't be written without at least a little bit of jargon. I'll do my best to explain as we go. For many of you, those explanations will be unnecessary, but others may welcome it. Basically, if a friend or family member who is *not* in a union has asked me a question, I'm going to assume a lot of you are asking it, too. In this case, the "private sector" is anyone who works for a business of some kind, while "public sector" means working for the government at the federal, state, local, or school district level. I know a fair number of people who have thought a company that is publicly traded on the stock market is in the public sector, so if you've made that mistake, rest assured you are not alone—no judgment.

grown accustomed to accepting that we were slowly on our way out, but that the fight was still worth having.

But for the last few years, something's different. Things have been looking . . . up.

Unions are more popular than ever. Gallup has long surveyed public opinion on unions, and their 70 percent favorability rating now is the highest it's been since 1965—and the numbers in 1965 were surely impacted by the fact that one in four of the respondents was currently in a union. While there are still plenty of Americans who practically worship the megarich like Elon Musk and Jeff Bezos, their union busting practices are the subject of scorn and derision. Few still believe the claim that, in the absence of unions, businesses will benevolently pay decent wages on their own.

You can see this everywhere. Take popular culture. A major network sitcom, *Superstore,* had a significant, multiseason plotline about the employees of the Walmart clone unionizing, with the union members placed in a sympathetic and at times heroic light. Jorts the Cat, the subject of a viral Reddit thread, now has an internet presence with hundreds of thousands of followers, and it turns out Jorts is wildly prounion, spreading his message of solidarity across the tubes. *Teen Vogue* (!) has run pieces by the former U.S. secretary of labor and by young workers who've organized their workplaces.

We were also fortunate, starting in 2021, to have economic conditions that were robustly proworker. President Biden's American Rescue Plan Act, and subsequent legislation, helped lead to the best employment numbers since the late 1990s, even if a severe inflationary cycle, and the ongoing disruptions of the world economy from war and COVID, don't always make things feel so good.[1] Demand for workers was high, and that gives workers more bargaining power than they've had in a long time. Under Biden—who was the first president ever to walk a union picket line—unions had a genuine champion in the White House. While that has changed, the impact of the Biden years on unions was unambiguously good.

Still, a strong economy and four years of a supportive government are no guarantee that workers will turn to unions to address low wages, unsafe workplaces, or the threats of new technology. But again and again in this book, we will see workers turn in the direction of solidarity, taking on corporations and bosses with purpose and commitment. Workers face moments of choice like this all the time: how to stand up to exploitative employers. For most of the last forty years, when presented with the chance to embrace solidarity, to stand together, the odds were better than even that workers would say no. They've clung to the individualism that's so deeply buried in our collective understanding of America: I'm better off on my own. No, I won't seek solidarity.

But in the last few years, they've said yes more and more. Workers who've never stood up are now jumping up not unlike the captured rebels at the end of the film *Spartacus*. They're organizing, they're striking, they're winning. Workers have always had a choice; it's just that now, more than ever, they're sticking with the union. They're discovering they have the power, and they've been using it.

This book is about those moments of choice, about how workers have leaned into solidarity in a way we haven't seen in generations.

This is not to say that the story of unions over the past fifty years has been one of unremitting sadness and defeat. Far from it. There have been powerful struggles, brilliant victories. Even at our weakest ebb, unions still have a lot of power and have used that power to make millions of lives better.

But it's also true that for every one of those amazing success stories, there have been even more setbacks. Defeats. Failures. We win a lot of battles but have been losing the war.

Until recently. This upsurge is different. It's not just a few isolated moments of glory; it's a sustained, synergistic, growing movement, and even the inauguration of a *very* antiunion Donald Trump may not be enough to slow it down. Victories are begetting other victories. Workers who have never met each other, who may live in different places, do different jobs, and be of different ages, skin colors, or nationalities, are now finding inspiration in each other, and are fighting *and winning* in ways that would have been unimaginable just a few years ago.

Why Now?

Gallup polls, full employment, and delightful internet cats are all well and good, but they simply aren't enough to explain why this is happening, and why now.

Understanding the *why* means trying to understand the workers themselves, who have been taking these great risks and winning greater victories. What's driving workers to act?

There are, of course, reasons specific to every individual worker, and to every unique workplace context, but this book is going to look at three particular factors. Listening to workers talk about their experiences, watching what has happened, these three things stand out above the others.

This first is the pandemic itself. Following upon a decade of stagnation after the Great Recession and the rise of Trumpism, COVID was the breaking point. It wasn't always—indeed it rarely was—about COVID itself. Rather, COVID was the catalyst, the *deus ex machina* that set the gears in motion. Politically, economically, socially, and culturally, the country was impacted deeply by the pandemic and our responses to it.

Emergencies and disasters, and our responses to them, regularly serve as inflection points in history. In particular, disasters and national traumas in recent decades have been used as excuses to hobble organized labor. In the 1940s, 1950s, 1960s, and even into the 1970s, America's unions, though far from perfect, spearheaded a period of unparalleled growth in the living standards of working people. It seemed as though the post-WWII economy would last forever, but starting in the 1970s, the other side took advantage of every opportunity to strike back, in a process Naomi Klein has dubbed Disaster Capitalism.[2]

The oil shock and inflationary spirals of the 1970s were accompanied by explicit efforts by policy makers to weaken the power of workers to demand higher wages. The Federal Reserve weaponized rate increases to increase unemployment and discipline labor, and Ronald Reagan took advantage of the moment to break the Professional Air Traffic Controllers' Organization (PATCO) in 1981, setting off a decade of union busting that devastated workers. Just in this century, we have time and again seen emergencies exploited by antiunion forces. The attacks of 9/11 led to a wave of Islamophobia and xenophobia that further divided the working class along racial lines. In 2005, right-wing lawmakers in Louisiana took advantage of the devastation of Hurricane Katrina to dismantle the New Orleans public school system, destroying in the process the strongest teachers union in the South—the New Orleans Federation of Teachers. The Great Recession's "bailout" of the auto industry slashed workers' pensions and health care benefits while setting the stage for the companies to earn a quarter-trillion dollars in profits over the next decade. And the Koch Brothers, former Wisconsin governor Scott Walker, and their right-wing allies used the Tea Party revolt to enact sweeping antiunion policies in state after state, as unions reeled back in confusion, unable to stem the tide.

COVID could easily have been more of the same. And, yet, it wasn't. All of us faced health risks, all of us faced economic disruption. Some of us had to take COVID head-on in the workplace. Those workers—including Frito-Lay workers in Kansas, classroom educators, and flight attendants—didn't have the luxury to stay home. The first section of the book will be about the intersections between their work and the pandemic. Working through COVID could have led them to despair and collapse, but instead these workers and their unions rose to the challenge and scored great victories for their members *and* for all of us.

The second factor is the impact of younger workers. Solidarity is a choice, and younger workers are embracing that choice with an enthusiasm and (importantly) a confidence that is surprising and impressive. I don't know how many meetings I've sat in where one union leader after another complained about how "the young people" just didn't appreciate the union, didn't care how much the union had won for them. If those leaders are still saying that, they have blinders on. The second section of this book will look specifically at two different places where younger workers are organizing with speed, sophistication, and strength: the explosion of organizing by graduate student workers, and the already-legendary Starbucks campaign. Well-informed, reasonably expert opinion* would have told anyone who listened, in 2016 or 2017, that neither of these organizing explosions was possible. Thank goodness we were wrong.

The third factor, which makes up the final section of this book, has been the surprising rejuvenation of some of America's most storied unions. Union members, seeing both the dangers and the opportunities of the moment, took the chance on new leadership at two unions where the old guard had held on for decades: the Teamsters and the United Auto Workers (UAW). At a third union, the Screen Actors Guild–American Federation of Television and Radio Artists (SAG-AFTRA), the union's leaders put aside deep personal and political animosities to unite in the face of real threats to their work. In 2023, two of these three unions went on strike, and all three of them won contract victories that exceeded our wildest imaginations. They proved that this upsurge isn't about just the popularity of unions, but that unions still have the power to make massive, fundamental improvements in the lives of their members.

---

* Mine and that of the labor people I talk to.

The common thread of all of these, to make the point again, is the choice to embrace solidarity. The struggles highlighted in this book all depended for success not just on leadership, but on regular working people thinking it over and deciding that the rational, best choice was to link arms and stand together. I'm in the labor movement because I always think that's the best decision, but I'm happily surprised to see so many workers agreeing with me.

Before going any further, it seems like it might be worth taking just a minute to walk through the bizarre world of the American labor movement, because it's an odd and at times confusing landscape and I don't want you to get too lost.

The Varieties of American Unionism

If you're not a member of a union, or you're a member of one but don't really know much about unions outside of your own workplace, the House of Labor can seem pretty daunting to comprehend. That's mostly because it is. Today's unions are built on Gilded Age foundations shaped by mid-twentieth-century labor laws and decades of swirling economic change. And nothing is the same everywhere. For everything you learn about unions, there's an exception. And another one. And probably eight or nine more.

Let's start with the organizations themselves. Unions come in all shapes and sizes, and we can't address them all, but they generally are composed of at least two parts. The big part, the headquarters of a whole union, is referred to as the international union, or just international. This name is one-half nineteenth-century socialist aspirational wishing (the goal being a labor movement that knew no national borders), and the other half the reality that many internationals are, indeed, international. Many of our unions have members in other countries and continents, though we are mostly going to ignore them in this book.

These internationals have many different names, and it doesn't help that sometimes the shorthand doesn't really seem like their real name. For example, the United Association of Journeymen and Apprentices of the Plumbing and Pipefitting Industry of the United States and Canada (UA), is generally just called the Plumbers, which is obviously leaving a lot out.* An even greater challenge is that the name of the union often tells you little about who it represents. The majority of the members of the United Auto Workers (UAW) don't work for a car manufacturer. The American Federation of Teachers (AFT) represents a lot of teachers, but also nurses and state government workers. The Teamsters, as they like to say themselves, represent everyone from airline pilots to zookeepers.

Most but not all American internationals are allied together in the American Federation of Labor–Congress of Industrial Organizations (AFL-CIO). The AFL-CIO, therefore, is not in and of itself a union; the often-used phrase that it is a "union of unions" is close enough for our purposes. Each and every international joins the AFL-CIO of its own volition, and the AFL-CIO has little power to compel any international to do anything. If an international doesn't like what the AFL-CIO is doing, they can leave, as several large unions did in 2005. Labor critics who say "the AFL-CIO should . . ." often have no idea how little power the organization has.

Indeed, even the internationals are limited in what they can do, because in the U.S. labor movement, the real power lies in union locals. A "local" can mean anything from fifteen bus drivers in central Missouri to a 250,000-person entity covering five states and hundreds of workplaces in scores of industries. In general, though, a local tends to refer to a group of workers who work for the same employer and are covered by the same union contract. That is, it's

---

* This challenge is best represented, perhaps, in the name of Homer Simpson's union: the International Brotherhood of Jazz Dancers, Pastry Chefs, and Nuclear Technicians.

the union for your locality, so it usually means what you'd guess it would mean. Locals usually have a number—sometimes just random, but sometimes with a special significance. The Chicago Teachers Union (CTU) is AFT Local 1, for example, because the AFT was founded in Chicago, though no one calls it Local 1, they call it CTU.

What do unions do? The main function of American unions is *collective bargaining.* It's sometimes said that it's illegal for some workers (especially in conservative states) to form unions, but that's untrue. Everyone in the United States has a constitutional right to free association with their fellow workers, and they have a right to call it a union. What they may or may not have is the right to collective bargaining. Collective bargaining is legal right established (or not), depending on where you work, by one of dozens of different laws.

Here's the basic version of how it works: Workers in a workplace decide they want a union. They sign union cards (usually called authorization cards) saying they want a specific union to represent them. The laws vary, but once they reach a certain threshold (usually 30 percent of the workers) they can file the cards with a relevant labor board, like the National Labor Relations Board. That board then oversees a secret-ballot election among the workers. If the workers vote for the union, then the union becomes the representative of those workers, and the employer is *legally bound* to negotiate with the union. The outcome of those negotiations is the contract, also called the collective bargaining agreement.

It's this legal requirement to negotiate that defines the bulk of what unions do: negotiate and enforce contracts. Contracts between unions and employers are usually enforced via grievance procedures—a process laid out in each contract, where the union represents the impacted worker(s). Most contractual grievance procedures end with arbitrations—a sort-of courtroom-looking procedure with a labor arbitrator instead of a judge. This work is not usually the stuff we talk a lot about, but it matters. That work also requires resources, so unions charge dues, anywhere from half a percent to 3 percent of a member's wages. Dues also support a union's other activities, like helping other people form unions. There are various restrictions on how unions can use dues money for politics, but there are plenty of ways to do so, and unions are definitely involved in politics.

Unions used to have the right to impose what was called the *closed shop*, meaning that only union members could be hired by the employer. That obviously gave the unions a lot of power, and so the opponents of unions got rid of that in the Taft-Hartley Act of 1947. Today, many private-sector unions have what's called a *union shop*, which means that while the employer can hire whomever it wants, that person, once on board, has to either join the union or pay a fee to cover the costs of the union's representational work.* In about half the country (mostly along a fairly familiar red state–blue state divide), unions cannot institute the union shop. Instead, they have the *open shop*, where unions are legally bound to represent all the workers, but a worker has a choice whether or not to join the union.† This is also the case for all public-sector union workers; many of them had union shop rights until the 2018 Supreme Court case *Janus v AFSCME* took them all away.

The last big thing to understand is that bosses—corporations large and small, and plenty of politicians, too—fight unions tooth and claw, every step of the way. This means they are always looking to find ways to weaken unions and take away their rights. These forces are very, very good at coming up with names to cover what

---

* There are a handful of interesting exceptions in construction and in ports and a few other places, but don't make me go there, please.
† Many union folk refer to people represented by unions but who do not pay union dues as freeloaders and while I'm sympathetic to that term, and really do think everyone ought to join their union, it's sometimes easy to forget that the real opponent is not your fellow workers, it's the bosses.

they're doing, but, at the core of it, the question they are fighting over is this one: *Who decides?*

Corporate America wants to decide for itself. Some openly desire to impoverish workers by paying them less and less and treating them worse and worse, but there is also a breed of boss that claims a desire to treat all workers well but that the union is getting in the way of being able to do the right thing. All that means is that the boss wants to make the decisions wholly unfettered. Any time you hear proposals for labor reform or hear about "disruptors" who want to "innovate," remember to look at the question of *who decides*. If the answer is "the boss," all the rest of the words don't matter.

I've been in the labor movement twenty-five years, and I'm constantly discovering little nooks and crannies of the institutional labor movement that I didn't know. I've done my best in this book to make things clear and hope you'll be able to navigate your way through it.

Much to my surprise, over the past few years I've found myself becoming an optimist about labor's future, and this, intentionally, is an optimistic book. We shouldn't pretend that everything is rosy, however. The racial reckoning brought on by George Floyd's murder included many heated conversations about police unions, and unions have much work to do to address racism in their own ranks and to build racial equity everywhere. Too many unions have been too open to the nativist xenophobia of the MAGA movement, choosing to believe the migrant worker, not the worker-crushing billionaire, is somehow the real threat. These unions might take deeply regrettable actions under the Trump presidency. If some of these frustrating and disappointing aspects of today's unions get less attention here, it is primarily because such disappointment isn't new, but the optimism is.

This book will focus tightly on workers at work and in their unions. This means that lots of very important subjects relevant to working people, including ones in which unions played a role, will be given less attention. I thought it better to have a tighter focus for the book than to range over too much ground, especially into areas where, frankly, I don't know enough to have useful things to say. As such, national politics will appear only rarely, with the exception of noting, repeatedly, that the Biden administration was the most prounion presidency since the death of Franklin Roosevelt. International affairs will also be largely absent; while unions often took public stances on, and their members were deeply impacted by, the Russian invasion of Ukraine and the Israel-Gaza conflict, for example, they're largely absent from these pages.

Even within my chosen scope there are so many stories that deserve to be told but won't be given as much attention here, because my publishers weren't keen on a million-word book. Some are covered in recent work by other authors. We're in a golden age of labor journalism—so golden that I originally wanted to write a whole chapter on media organizing but had to cut it for space—and there are brilliant journalists and writers out there whose names you'll find in my endnotes and whom you should really check out.

This book is, to no small degree, a hostage to fortune. There is every possibility that the tide will turn in the Trump years, that unions will be forced back into long, slow retreats, and this moment in time will be just that—a moment, here today, gone tomorrow. I really don't think that it matters. If this is the beginning of something amazing, it'll have been important to have a record of that starting point. If it's just another somewhat bigger blip, that takes nothing away from the courage and genius and power we'll see in these pages. The story is worth telling no matter what the ending will be.

Part I:
The Breaking Point

We all lived through it. Thinking back, though, it's remarkable how quickly everything changed. For most of us, anyway.

In a flash, restaurants closed. Bars closed. Hair salons. Movie theaters. Heck, all theaters. Schools. Colleges. So much more.

The world had never seen anything like it. Individual areas, hit by a hurricane or a earthquake, or devastated by war, certainly have had it worse, where closure of businesses was coupled with massive physical devastation. But the whole country, all at once? The whole world?

On Friday the thirteenth of March, 2020, I had a grievance arbitration hearing for a union member who'd gotten the shaft. We joked about the coronavirus, but it didn't feel real. By the next week, we were shut down. I lost the case.

When the pandemic lockdowns hit, workers split into three relatively distinct groups. The first group, which also was the whitest and the wealthiest group, were office workers and other white-collar jobs that shifted to full-time remote work. We turned kitchen tables and basements into makeshift home offices, and experienced, for the first time, telling someone they were on mute when they tried to speak on Zoom.

Those in the second group lost their jobs as places closed down—more than 20 million additional unemployed workers in just two weeks. It was scary for all, but far less bad than it could have been. The Democratic Congress persuaded Trump (who's never cared a fig for actual policy and just wanted credit for doing something) to sign a bill implementing a massive increase in unemployment insurance, covering more workers than ever before, and making benefits far more generous. For the time being, in 2020, the vast majority of unemployed workers had a genuine safety net protecting them. Corporations also had guaranteed profits, of course.

The third group had to stay working. They put on masks, washed their hands a lot, and hoped. Bosses went through the motions of rearranging things for social distancing. For a while they got called heroes. But talk is cheap. We did not treat them as heroes. During the initial lockdown and beyond, the workers who had to stay on the job—to keep us fed, to keep us healthy, to educate our kids, to see us from place to place—never had a respite from the pandemic.

The rest of us were happy to sacrifice them so long as it meant we weren't too terribly inconvenienced. Through the pandemic's first couple of years, especially, Americans showed a remarkable degree of contempt for frontline workers.

No wonder they hit their breaking point. No wonder some of them took action.

But not just for themselves. The unifying experience of the pandemic, where people banded together to look out for each other because no one could escape it, is reflected in the kinds of actions taken by frontline workers and their unions: unselfish, with a conscious eye out for helping the whole community.

From Frito-Lay workers in Topeka, to teachers in Chicago and the flight attendants flying in the air above us all, frontline workers practiced the core value that the labor movement teaches: that we struggle not just for ourselves, or for our friends or family, but for millions more whose names we will never know, whose stories we will never hear, and who in turn will never know who it was whose actions reached out and helped them.

Fighting for people you'll never know. We call that solidarity.

1

Worked to the Bone

As we settled into our homes during the first wave of the pandemic, we all had different ways of coping. For me it was Cheetos.

The challenge with Cheetos has always been the dust—that delicious orange dust that sticks to your fingers and lips, coats your tongue, and stubbornly resists efforts to remove it. It's hard to eat Cheetos in lots of settings. Makes you look unprofessional.

The pandemic was perfect for Cheetos consumption, especially in those early months before we all upgraded our web cameras. No one would even notice. So I ate Cheetos. A lot.

This chapter is about the workers who produced those Cheetos, and how they fought back when the demands on their time and their bodies were too much. The first major strike of the COVID era was at the Frito-Lay plant in Topeka, Kansas. It could have been a flash in the pan. Instead, it lit up the country, touching off worker actions across America's heartland.

You often meet folks who worked in food production and will never, ever eat the product they produced, because they know too much about how it was made. Talk to the workers at Frito-Lay—members of the Bakery, Confectionery, Tobacco Workers and Grain Millers International Union (BCTGM), Local 218, in Topeka—though, and it's the opposite. Esther Fanning makes SunChips. "We take a lot of pride in the product we make," she says. If there's even a slight error, "We feel so guilty." Frito-Lay workers know that they're professionals doing a really good job.

The chips you munch are the product of an elaborate, precise process that is a marvel to behold. The whole thing is just fascinating. Frito-Lay continues to add more and more machinery, but far from turning the work into robotic drudgery, it demands even more skill and care from the workers. There's a lab on-site where every ingredient is tested, generally every day but sometimes even more often, for impurities, imperfections, and variations in taste, texture, and density. Operators of the cookers, the grinders, the ovens, and the fryers have to be on constant lookout for any minor change—an oven too hot, a fryer too cool—and they are trained to spring into action immediately to fix any small problems. Is the chip not airy enough? Too airy? Is the seasoning evenly distributed across all chips? Is the color just right? Is the balance of ingredients exactly as it should be? The standard is that every chip they make should have the same qualities, exactly. Nothing less is acceptable.

This means the BCTGM members must be ever vigilant and know how to respond to dozens of possible scenarios. They need to have smooth communication up and down the line, because a hold-up in one place throws everything off balance.

Until July 2021 there had never been a strike. Never even been close. But working during the pandemic proved to be too much. The workers weren't willing to take it.

The American myth includes a belief that there was some period of time when most of our food was produced by small farmers who owned and worked their own land, then sent what they made to the miller and the butcher and the baker, who made it into bread and chicken fingers and double cheeseburgers and Cheetos.

This was never really true. Food production has always been dangerous work. The workers have always been underpaid, uncared for, exploited. And, for most of American history, we've been content to let them suffer, so long as we got our Cheetos.

Upton Sinclair's *The Jungle*, published in 1906, was one of the first works to draw attention to the horrific conditions in food industries—in his case, meatpacking. If you were taught about *The Jungle* in high school Social Studies, you probably learned that it helped lead to the passage of laws like the Pure Food and Drug Act, which made food safer to eat. Unless you had an exceptional teacher, though, you maybe didn't notice that it didn't lead to any laws designed to protect the *workers* in those meatpacking plants. It was fine if meatpackers lost a few fingers, so long as those fingers were mostly kept out of the ground beef.

Indeed, right at the time *The Jungle* came out, protections for food workers were struck a serious blow by the Supreme Court's infamous *Lochner* decision.[1] New York had taken the drastic, anarchist-inspired, revolution-heralding decision to pass a law restricting the hours of work for bakery employees to a mere sixty a week. The nerve. The Supreme Court struck it down as interfering in the right of a worker to negotiate their own contract with an employer on mutually agreeable terms.* It was far easier to pass legislation aimed at protecting *consumers* than workers. It still is.

Suicide Shifts at Frito-Lay

And so we can eat our favorite snack chips with the knowledge that laws are in place to help keep us safe. And all of us needed Cheetos—or whatever it was you used—to cope in the spring of 2020, because COVID threw everyone's lives into disarray. In the first week of March 2020, about 200,000 people filed for unemployment benefits, a normal number—if anything, a bit low. Three

---

* We're going to see this particular phenomenon a *lot* in this book—courts, lawmakers, bosses, and journalists ignoring the power dynamics at play between a worker and a boss, acting as if a single worker (outside of rare examples like professional athletes or Tom Cruise) has the power to negotiate with the boss as an equal. They have to ignore it, because if you say it out loud you just sound silly.

weeks later it was *6 million*. The U.S. economy had never seen so many people thrown out of work so quickly.

Usually, when people lose their jobs, their spending declines precipitously. Unemployment benefits cover only some of the lost income, and so workers losing their jobs can lead to other businesses losing their income, leading them to lay off workers, and around we go. Not this time.

There is no more damning criticism of so-called free-market capitalism than how quickly it gets abandoned when things go bad. While the Republican Party and its pro-business financiers had kept the minimum wage stuck at $7.25 for more than a decade, the pandemic threw that out the window as new legislation added $600 a week to unemployment benefits: Unemployed workers were now making $15 an hour. Stimulus checks went to millions. Self-employed workers and independent contractors got access to unemployment insurance. An eviction and foreclosure moratorium went into place. Paid leave was introduced to help people care for family members. For a brief period of time, we had a social safety net on par with the most generous Scandinavian countries. It really boggles the mind how hard our political leaders have tried to get us to forget that.

What did we do with this robust safety net? We bought *stuff*. But not just any stuff. Our spending was shaped by the circumstances of the pandemic. In particular, because most restaurants were closed, and more of us were at home (remote working or laid off), we bought a lot of Cheetos. And ice cream. And cookies. And meat and cheese and veggies and fruit and nuts and everything else.

Topeka, Kansas, has one of the largest snack-producing facilities in the country. Doritos, Cheetos, Tostitos, Lay's Potato Chips, SunChips, Fritos, and more are made by workers represented by BCTGM Local 218. Local 218 was founded in 1898. The Topeka Frito-Lay plant was unionized in 1972.

It's not too surprising that it took seventy-four years. Workers who produce the food we eat have long tried to organize and have long had a difficult time. Racism and xenophobia are two of the biggest reasons.

Farmworkers laboring in the fields have had it the worst. One of the signature pieces of Franklin Delano Roosevelt's New Deal, for example, was the Fair Labor Standards Act of 1938 which undid *Lochner* and implemented the nation's first minimum wage and overtime protections. It excluded farmworkers. Farmworkers were also excluded from the right to collective bargaining in the National Labor Relations Act, and from unemployment insurance protections and Social Security.

Then and now you sometimes see blather about how farmworkers have particularly unique working conditions, and federal law just isn't equipped with the flexibility to blah blah blah. FDR needed the votes of Southern senators to pass New Deal laws. Most farmworkers in the South were Black. The Southern senators didn't want to help Black workers, so they kept them (and domestic workers, too) out of the bill. This wasn't some kind of great secret at the time—it was clearly and obviously the reason to anyone who was paying attention.[2]

Sadly, it wasn't just Southern white politicians. Unions themselves also have an ugly history of racism, and also of discrimination against immigrants. In Topeka, at Frito-Lay, this manifested itself in a divide between white and Latino workers in the plant. There wasn't, as far as I can tell, outright hostility or conflict, but workers knew which side of the divide they were on, and as long as that divide persisted, it was something the bosses could use against them. It's always been that way.

Here's a party game for you: The next time you're with a bunch of friends who think of themselves as prolabor, ask them the name of the first piece of federal legislation passed through the efforts of the American labor movement. They'll guess the right to organize unions, or the minimum wage, that sort of thing. You, then, can take all the fun out of the room by telling them the answer: The Chinese Exclusion Act of 1882—a law intended to keep Chinese immigrants from coming to America and barring them from employment opportunities when they did. It was not the last time labor unions used their political power against immigrants.

This is a book celebrating labor unions, so it's fitting that here in this first chapter we acknowledge that labor unions have often been (and sometimes still are) racist, sexist, and xenophobic.[3] There's never been an excuse for it, and throughout labor history there are examples of labor leaders who knew it was wrong and fought against it, so "they didn't know any better" isn't a valid defense.

The biggest problem at Frito-Lay—the one without which there surely wouldn't have been this strike—was the suicide shifts. Directed to stay four hours late after one shift, then called in four hours early for the next one, workers had only eight hours off to go home, eat, shower, sleep, say hello to their families, pay bills, or just do nothing for a little while before having to come back to work for another twelve hours.

Even when they weren't assigned suicide shifts, most of the workers were facing twelve-hour days, seven days a week. For weeks and weeks and weeks in a row. We've all met those braggarts who claim they work eighty- or ninety-hour weeks at a financial firm or law office. Even if they're telling the truth (which, let's be honest, they're not), it's a very different kind of eighty hours. You get up and walk around when you need to. You step into the break room and spend half an hour discussing the NCAA basketball tournament. You're sitting most of the time, in a climate-controlled environment, with a fair amount of autonomy on the job.

Frito-Lay workers didn't have those kinds of eighty-four-hour weeks. They had on-your-feet, working-with-dangerous-machinery eighty-four-hour weeks. Bruni Torrez remembers being mortified when people asked her kids what they did together with their mother. "Mom sleeps." Bruni's kids were growing up without her. "You see your children," said Esther Fanning, "and they're doing something you had no idea about. . . . You're there, but you're not there."

And the money wasn't keeping up. For years, Frito-Lay had been *the* manufacturing job to have in Topeka, but not anymore. Cheri Renfro's hourly rate of pay, over the previous ten years before the strike, had gone up all of thirty cents. Not thirty cents a year—thirty cents total over ten years. During those same ten years, the stock price of PepsiCo—Frito-Lay's parent company—had almost doubled. And the whole plant, with over 850 workers, had just one payroll person, so workers were constantly finding their checks were wrong, holidays calculated incorrectly, overtime missing, so even the wages they did earn didn't always make it into their pockets.

The working conditions were also deteriorating. Pleasant Desch is a third-shift sanitation lead. Unlike some places, "sanitation" at Frito-Lay isn't just another word for mopping floors. Pleasant and her crew make sure every single surface that food touches is cleaned and sterilized, multiple times a day. They do this using CIP—Clean In Place—meaning the work of the factory doesn't stop as they clean. It requires speed, precision, and thoroughness. Even a tiny bit of contamination can shut down the line for hours.

Sanitation isn't soap and water. They use caustic and acidic chemicals in massive quantities. Take the fryers, for example. They're the size of small rooms, in which hundreds of gallons of oil fry a lifetime's worth of corn chips in minutes. To clean that fryer, you need to boil caustic chemicals in it that heat up and sanitize every square millimeter. Pleasant's sanitation crew wears masks, full body suits, gloves, and ventilators.

And it's hot. The facility has no central climate control. In the winter it's freezing. In the summer it's broiling. It can get up to 140 degrees in the hottest parts of the buildings. Imagine that in a hazmat suit;

even in the middle of winter, it's hot in those suits. Pleasant bought, out of her own pocket, ice vests for her crew to wear and keeps her own personal medicine cabinet stocked with rapid hydration tablets, pain relievers, and allergy medicine. And in that heat, in those suits, they have to engage in precision cleaning work, mistake-free.

I often wonder, when I hear about workers doing seventy- or eighty-hour weeks someplace, why the company just doesn't hire more. The thing is, though, you have to get them to stay. Training for most of the jobs at Frito-Lay took weeks or even months, and lots and lots of workers wouldn't stick it out. Between the temperature swings and the long hours and the lack of raises, the company was trying to hire, but they couldn't. Mark Benaka was the business agent for Local 218 at the time of the strike. "They hire ten people this week; by the end of the month, three of them might still be there. They would walk out on their lunches and not come back to work."

By the summer of 2021, the economy was roaring back in style, and people who didn't like the work could find better jobs with little trouble.* Suicide shifts were more and more common, and people were getting angry.

Strike!

Pay matters. Hours matter. Safety matters. But even the most egregious workplace problems usually don't lead to strikes. The folks at Frito-Lay weren't the only people in the country, or even in their city, working suicide shifts. To get workers to the point where they are ready to act, you need one more thing.

---

* This has commonly been referred to as the Great Resignation, but that's entirely wrong. People weren't quitting a job and leaving the workforce; they were quitting one job and taking another, better, one. The parade of business owners who rent their garments and complained "No one wants to work anymore" were telling on themselves. No one wanted to work for *them*. It's much better to call it the Great Reallocation.

"You get companies that just don't respect you and don't treat you like a human being," said Cheri Renfro. "And that's when you got to stand up and say, 'Hey, enough's enough.'"

Pleasant Desch knew workers who'd gotten into car accidents, falling asleep driving home after seven twelve-hour days, and "the company didn't care."

"We are sacrificing," said Fanning, "and there was no recognition. It was a never-ending cycle. . . . It was just too much."

It's all about respect.

Companies never learn this. I've had bosses laugh out loud when we tell them the workers want respect. It's a genuine mystery to me why they don't get it, but mostly they don't. And when you have deteriorating working conditions, low pay, and long hours, and you throw a lack of basic common decency into the mix, it can light the fire.

Mark Benaka, now in retirement, credits the newer, younger workers for driving it forward. They kept pushing for the union to make bigger demands at the bargaining table. Like a lot of old-timers, when younger workers began agitating for more and more, he remembered back to his younger days. He'd wanted to push for more when he was younger, too, but it never went anywhere; it didn't work. But this new group of younger workers "kept pushing harder and harder and harder. As it turned out, it was a good thing." Mark had clearly done some reflecting in the years since the strike. "It didn't seem right to us old-timers; that wasn't the culture we were raised in." He's pleased to have been wrong. Sadly, not all union leaders are as willing to acknowledge mistakes.

It was the younger workers, too, who helped bridge the plant's longstanding racial divide between white workers and Latino workers. When it comes to food workers, action really only happens when there is unity across racial and ethnic groups.

Often, it was migrant workers who led this charge. Take Hawaii, for example. Hawaii's status as the most union-dense state in the country hails back to the interracial cooperation of Japanese and Filipino laborers, fighting exploitation on sugar plantations in the first years of the twentieth century.[4]

Efforts at unity haven't always gone as well. Organizing work by sharecroppers in the South in the hundred years after the Civil War, for example, often led to violence by white authorities directed at the workers, including lynchings. Those authorities were particularly scared because some of those efforts involved white and Black sharecroppers working together. Strikes in other parts of the country were broken up by private mercenaries hired by large landowners; because farms were often far away from towns and cities, striking farmworkers had to camp on open ground, making them vulnerable to attacks and blockades to starve them out.[5] John Steinbeck's 1936 novel, *In Dubious Battle*, is a fictionalization of the California farmer strikes during the 1930s that highlights how worker unity in the face of racist attacks was necessary for action. Fitting for a novel about the Depression, it's pretty depressing.*

The workers at Frito-Lay pushed through these divides and focused their ire on their employer. The union negotiated a contract and brought it to the membership, who voted it down. They reached a second agreement, and the workers voted it down. Then they voted to strike. Indeed, lots of workers, including Pleasant Desch, joined the union just so they could vote to go on strike.

And so, on July 5, the day after the holiday, BCTGM Local 218 walked off the job.

What does it mean to go on strike? At the most basic level, it means you stop coming to work. Your power over the company is that your labor is what makes its profits, so if you withhold your

---

* Don't cheat and watch the 2016 movie starring James Franco—it departs substantially from the book, telling a very, very different story.

labor, you hurt its bottom line and its incentive to reach a deal goes up. But going on strike is also inflicting pain on yourself. Your income is what allows you to thrive. The union usually helps with strike pay and some states allow strikers to collect unemployment insurance. But to some degree, it's a race—your ability to hold out versus the company's.*

If you've never been on strike, think of it as one part theme-park haunted house, one part waiting in line at the DMV, one part spring break, and one part storming the castle. They're not equal-sized parts, though, and the strikes that work are the ones that get the proportions right.

A strike is scary. There's no getting around it. You don't know what's coming next and it's the not knowing that causes the most anxiety. You've put your job on the line, your family's livelihood. You have to trust that your co-workers—many of whom you've never really met before—are going to stick with you through the scariest bits, and not run away.

A strike is also truly, agonizingly boring. You spend most of your time walking a picket line, carrying a sign,† your shoulder getting tired and your feet wearing out. Not much changes to liven up your day, and there's little prospect of things being any different tomorrow. It's the kind of boredom where you start to get snippy with people around you, snapping at the smallest things, just to have a reason to feel something.

A strike is also a party. You never run out of food on the picket

---

* As we will see in later chapters, sometimes this "classic" kind of strike isn't possible—like when the boss is a school district and there are no profits to stop, or when it is an insufficient tactic all by itself. The Frito-Lay strike, however, was very much an old-school type of economic strike.

† If you take only one thing from this book, I want it to be this: *Put duct tape on the handles of your picket signs.* I don't know why, but it's magic. Hold a wooden or plastic handle for more than ten minutes, and your hand feels irritated and uncomfortable. A thin piece of duct tape on that handle and you can carry that thing all day. Seriously. Masking tape in a pinch, but duct tape is best.

line, and while there's usually healthy stuff like apples or trail mix, there's also an infinite sea of donuts and pizza. Like at a big, long party, they get stale sometimes, but they're still pretty good. And you're hanging with your comrades. Often there's music, and if there's not music, you can make music from the car horns of supporters as they drive by. You come up with silly chants and dumb picket-line games to help you pass the time. Sometimes, you end up alone with someone, and you pour your heart out to each other, and the next day you act like it didn't happen.

But it's a party with a purpose. You have a mission. It's a conflict, and those in the fight with you will be special to you for the rest of your life. *We few, we happy few,* says Shakespeare's Henry V, and that's really what it is. For anyone who's been on strike, it's one of the signal moments, the most transcendent, of their lives. You always remember who was with you. Talk to people who went on strike twenty, thirty, or forty years ago, and they'll remember it as if it had ended the week before.

There's a lot more to winning a strike than the picket line, of course: Bargaining tactics and legal strategies to push the levers of power your way. Appeals to the media, the public, politicians. Resisting the company's attempts to get injunctions to stop your picket lines, to let them run in strikebreakers without interference. All those matter, and may indeed matter more than the picket line. But if you're the regular worker on strike, not a leader at the negotiating table or a media liaison or whatever, the experience of the picket line matters a great deal.

And the workers at BCTGM Local 218 nailed the picket line.

Shane Nichols was there every single night. The strike lasted three weeks, but he went home only two or three times. He brought a big combo grill and they cooked food on the line. After a few days, he lost his voice, so he rigged up two train horns and would blow them every time a bus bearing strikebreakers came to the gate. The police came to talk to him about it, but it wasn't a residential area so there was no noise complaint. It just made him move the horn closer to the gate so the bus drivers would really hear it when they came in.

A lot of the strikers were Latino and the grills on the picket lines made burritos as well as hot dogs and burgers. There were coolers with beer in them. The owner of a vacant lot across the street from the plant ("Very strong Republican, very Trump-ish," said Benaka) let them use the lot for free as long as they cleaned up. They started sending flying squads to the stores around town, taking pictures of empty shelves and posting them on Facebook to show the impact the strike was having. "We were all out there for different reasons," said Desch. "Everybody had their own dog in the fight. But we were all out there to support one another."

Frito-Lay didn't take this lying down. All day, every day, the workers saw buses of strikebreakers pull into the plant. Twenty, thirty buses a day. There was the fear of the unknown: How much work were they getting done, how much were they producing? Would the company be able to wait out the strike and continue to make profits?

Modern technology took the sting out of that fear, though. One of the strikers owned a drone with an ultra-high-definition camera. They launched it from the parking lot and flew it over the plant. The buses had been pulling out of sight before they opened their doors and the drone showed that the buses were full of . . . nothing. The company had been running empty buses throughout the day, to give the impression of a huge number of replacements. They also used the drone to monitor the trains coming in with raw materials; deliveries were slow. They knew the plant wasn't keeping up with our insatiable demand for Cheetos.

Not everyone went on strike. Managers and supervisors had to stay on the job. Bruni Torrez was good friends with one, who called her on the picket line to ask for one of the computer passwords. "I'm like, 'I'm sorry, too bad.'"

It wasn't only managers, though. Nearly half the workers stayed on the job. "People needed health insurance for their kids," noted Renfro, sympathetically. Workers would be on the picket line one day and back in the plant on the next. Some of the workers who'd talked the toughest leading up to the strike didn't stop working. That was tough to bear.

But they bore it, for three long weeks. Then, it was over.

An Ending and a Beginning

The old line is that it's easy to go out on strike but hard to come back in. Everyone digs in the longer the strike lasts. Every day adds more grievances to the pile, more demands you want to see resolved. It's a tough balancing act for the union's leadership. You want to aim high, to keep your members enthused about staying out by promising to fight for the big things, but you also know that the goal is a *deal,* one that both sides can live with. It's rare to find such a deal that doesn't leave some members disappointed.

On July 23, members voted 200–178 to accept the deal and end the strike. It had squeaked by. Many were hoping for more. "I was hoping to get a little bit farther, especially with wages," said Renfro.[6] After thirty cents in ten years, she got an additional forty cents a year—a large change compared to the past, but still not a lot. "But I'm still glad we did it," she said, "The contract we have now, it's not the best but it's . . ."

"A lot better," finished Torrez.

They won an end to suicide shifts, and a guaranteed day off each week for every worker. They won bereavement leave, and an increase in vacation time. No one I talked to called it a marvelous victory. But most called it enough.

Because the negotiations process had dragged on so long even before the strike, Frito-Lay and BCTGM were back at the bargaining table for the next contract almost immediately. The balance of power was different now; a strike was no longer a theoretical possibility but a present threat. The union won an 11 percent raise, a $1,500 signing bonus, extra parental leave, a bigger shift differential,* and more.

In the wake of the strike, Pleasant Desch, Esther Fanning, and others became union stewards, deepening their commitment to their members. "People are not scared," says Fanning. "That fear is not there anymore."

There were moments of tension as the strikers came back in to face those who hadn't gone on strike. Bruni Torrez didn't think she could even speak to them, but Jason Davis, the union's international representative who'd helped with the strike,† made the case: "You need to go back and you need to try to earn [the trust of] these people because this fight is not over." Torrez has tried to stick with that. You can tell it's been hard.

It's always been hard for workers in food production, from the farm to the factory to the grocery store shelves and the restaurants. But still they organize.

In the 1960s, Cesar Chavez and the United Farm Workers ran a legendary, powerful campaign to win union rights for tens of thousands of migrant workers on farms in California's Salinas Valley.[7] Recognizing that people think of food through the lens of consumers, the UFW's grape boycott won them public sympathy, and in 1975 California passed a law granting farmworkers the right to collective bargaining.

---

* A shift differential is extra money to workers scheduled for different kinds of shifts—nights, weekends, holidays, etc.—in recognition that those shifts put increased burdens on people and their families.
† Union staff parachuted in from outside to help in strikes are often looked at with disdain by workers on the picket line, but the ones I spoke to had great admiration for Jason Davis. None of them had been on strike before, and he helped them get organized and figure out how to handle the myriad details that go into a successful walkout.

Farmworkers have in recent years seen both victories and setbacks. A huge march of farmworkers to Sacramento in 2022 persuaded Governor Gavin Newsom to sign an expansion of collective bargaining rights, but other states have failed to pass legislation guaranteeing farmworkers a minimum wage, protections from heat, or the right to water breaks. Federal law largely remains silent on farmworkers.

On the other end of the food production chain, the United Food and Commercial Workers (UFCW) union represents hundreds of thousands of grocery workers. UNITE-HERE represents workers in restaurants and bars.* An offshoot of UNITE-HERE, Workers United, now affiliated with the Service Employees International Union (SEIU), has led one of the most inspiring organizing campaigns of labor's resurgence: Starbucks Workers United (SBWU). We'll see a lot more of them in chapter 5.

Workers in the middle of the production chain—the plants where farm products are turned into the food we eat—have been organizing a long time, but it's difficult. More and more of that work is being done in so-called right-to-work states in the South and Midwest that mandate an open shop, which we discussed in the book's introduction. Those aren't states that are willing to pass laws to improve the health, safety, or compensation of food workers. Parts of the industry—like meatpacking, which used to have strong unions—were battered and weakened by a wave of corporate cutbacks and failed strikes in the 1980s and 1990s.[8]

Given that history, it's not a surprise that the Frito-Lay strike of July 2021 in Topeka sent shock waves across the food production industries. It uncorked the bottle: Discontent that had long been

---

* UNITE-HERE was formed in 2004 through the merger of two unions, the Union of Needletrades, Industrial, and Textile Employees (UNITE) and the Hotel Employees and Restaurant Employees Union (HERE). Bucking American labor tradition, their new name is not an acronym—it's just UNITE-HERE.

bubbling beneath the surface burst forth as workers saw Local 218 strike, win, and live to tell the tale.

Nabisco workers struck in August at facilities from Oregon to Georgia. It was their first strike since 1956. They won a $5,000 signing bonus, raises, increases to retirement contributions, and more. In October, the Kellogg Company's main facility in Battle Creek, Michigan, saw its first strike since 1972. The deal raised the minimum wage for new hires from under $22 an hour to over $24.[9] Ten thousand workers at John Deere in Illinois, members of the United Auto Workers, went on their first strike in more than three decades, winning an $8,500 signing bonus and a 10 percent raise the first year.

Would they all have walked out if BCTGM Local 218 hadn't? There's no way to know for sure, but I think the answer is clear. Success is contagious, and so is failure.

History is built on moments like the Local 218 strike.

If it had failed, if the workers had been beaten, there would have been no surprise expressed among the labor movement's talking heads. It's been rough for labor for decades, after all. Local 218 got only half the plant to strike. The company was too big and, with its deep pockets, waited them out. The pandemic made everyone scared about losing their health insurance. There would have been a million reasons why the strike was doomed from the start.

The pandemic had been raging for more than a year. Thousands were dying every week. Donald Trump had attempted a coup d'etat on January 6, 2021, and within days the whole Republican Party was lining up in support of people who'd wanted to overthrow the government by force (and we see how that turned out). Everything was out of balance.

But from the heartland of America, from Topeka, a ray of light, of hope, of solidarity. A reminder to us all that a better world is possible, that *labor omnia vincit.*

It was the first major strike of the pandemic era. The workers fought, won, and lived to tell the tale. It was a tipping point, the first movement in a symphony of solidarity that would sweep across every industry, every part of the country, and build worker power in ways we were not yet able to imagine.

2

Running Out of Adults in the Classroom

There was a brief moment of hope in the spring of 2021. Vaccines were rolling out. COVID case levels were dropping. It had been a rough year, but we had a new president committed to taking on the pandemic, and for a little while it seemed like it might work out. Maybe COVID would just . . . go away. Then the Republicans turned against vaccines and the Delta variant went wild on the whole world and it was clear it wasn't going to be that easy.

A lot of us, though, wanted to be done with the pandemic, and if that meant hurting some workers in the process, that's just the American Way.

Everyone experienced COVID in their own fashion, and there were parts of it that were worse for some people than others. Few, however, experienced things worse than did middle-class families. For they had been enduring the worst pain imaginable: *Their kids were home with them every day, and not at school.* The horror.

These suburban lawyers and accountants and real estate agents and financial something-or-others had bravely borne this burden through 2020 and the first half of 2021. They nobly sacrificed their dens for their kids' remote schooling. They bore with great dignity the incessant chatter of their children through the whole DAY instead of for just a few hours in the evening. Heroes, one and all.

But everyone has limits. And as the 2021–22 school year began, many of these middle-class parents decided they had suffered enough. It was time for someone else to watch their kids. It was time for them to go back to school.

Seizing upon often inaccurate, always incomplete, and frequently made-up data showing that, contrary to basic precepts of the germ theory of disease, schools were magically able to stop the coronavirus at the school door, they clamored to prevent learning loss by getting their kids off the couch and back to class. When the workers in those schools—represented by some of the country's largest unions—dared to suggest that maybe herding large numbers of young people into classrooms for six hours at a stretch was not always the smartest move, they were castigated as selfish, lazy, incompetent frauds, and their unions derided as barriers to progress.

Those educators fought back. Despite enduring a decade of the worst attacks unions have seen since the 1940s, educators in Chicago, Minneapolis, and elsewhere marched, struck, and organized to win basic protections on the job, and even got one of their own elected mayor of one of the nation's largest cities.

They did something more, too. They challenged one of the basic underlying foundations of collective bargaining in the United States.

Educating in a Pandemic: Won't *Someone* Think of the Children?

The key thing to remember, as we consider the debates around schooling during the pandemic, is that there weren't any *good* choices. There were bad choices and other bad choices, and the question was which was less bad. Remote schooling had serious limitations. The physical distance, the difficulty in reading body language of kids on tiny screens, the lack of group interaction all mattered. Kids in remote schooling also had a harder time accessing the many services they get from schools, like special education,

English-language learner content, school meals, extracurricular activities, and more. If kids came from households with poor internet access, their education suffered.

While the pandemic was raging, there were also significant downsides to having kids in school together. Children were far less likely to suffer serious consequences from COVID than adults, but they were still in danger. More significantly, though, was the danger to their families, because kids could easily pick up COVID at school and bring it home to more vulnerable adults. And, of course, the adults working in the school system, from the bus drivers who picked the kids up to the teachers and classroom assistants to the lunchroom staff were every bit as at-risk as other adults.

In reality, there was only one reasonable path forward. It was composed of two elements:

1. Do everything you can to make schools as safe as possible—improve air quality, set up classrooms to allow for social distancing, have a standard on-site test-and-trace regime, vaccinate everyone, and so forth; and,
2. Stay on top of caseloads in your community and be prepared to switch back to remote learning if things get bad.

As early as February 2021, this was precisely what the American Federation of Teachers (AFT), one of the nation's two major education unions, was saying. Their "Road Map to Safely Reopening Our Schools" reads like the most common of common sense. It recommends testing, masking, vaccines, accommodations for high-risk personnel, and safety committees. It also suggests that "communities need a metric for community infection rates that will trigger increasing safeguards, including temporary closures." [1]

Seems sensible enough.

How, then, did we get to the point where erstwhile GOP presidential candidate Mike Pompeo decided to say in 2022 that AFT president Randi Weingarten was the "most dangerous person in the world"?[2]

It makes much more sense when you remember the Law of Billionaire Public Policy Translation: *When a union takes a side in a public policy debate, the other side, irrespective of the nature of the original public policy issue, invariably changes its primary goal to that of the demonization and destruction of unions.*

COVID in the Classroom

"The first couple [of] months," recalled Chicago high school history teacher Eden McCauslin, "it was just nonstop sirens in the city." With everyone in their homes, there were rarely moments when children weren't hearing police cars, fire trucks, or ambulances through the microphone of another student, even if the siren was miles away from them. Schools across the country were struggling to figure out the basic technology of remote learning, which was more difficult in poorer neighborhoods where kids might have no internet access at home and might not even have a quiet room where they could focus on schooling.

For kids with special needs, it was especially challenging. Linda Perales, a special education teacher in Chicago, found that some of her students couldn't log in to a computer when their parents weren't home, because they didn't know how. Perales started assembling weekly packets for each student and delivering them to their homes in person, around town. "Parents, if they could, would sit right there with their student as we would go through a lesson," though some parents couldn't.

Linda was far from the only teacher to visit student homes outside of standard school hours, to make sure they were getting the best support she could provide, though it wasn't enough. Linda and the members of the Chicago Teachers Union's Latinx Caucus began raising their own money, "solidarity funds," to support families of kids who lacked the resources to support them during the pandemic.

Remember that the next time you hear about selfish teachers. Linda Perales and her colleagues were pooling their own money to help the families of their students. When you talk to educators about their work, they don't talk about their work. They talk about the kids. Students *are* the work.

Then, a new dimension hit. "In May, June," recalls McCauslin, "I started having kids saying my grandma died, or my grandpa died." It only got worse the next school year. "The deaths started piling up."

Students who were too young for the responsibility of caring for their younger siblings were given no choice. As more and more pandemic relief programs shut down, and more and more parents went back to work, students found themselves in the roles of parent, counselor, cook, nurse, and more. It wasn't just their siblings they cared for either, as sick grandparents or aunts and uncles began moving into homes, taking up space and adding to their burdens.

This was what educators across the country experienced. All educators have, at one point or another, had to help a student who lost a family member or a friend, or had one hospitalized, but those used to be rare occasions. Once or twice a year, maybe. Now it was all the time.

Some kids didn't understand what was going on. Their parents, perhaps out of a desire to spare them the worst of it, or maybe because it was just too much, weren't telling them what was going on. It fell on teachers to explain the pandemic while they were trying to teach.

Like the Frito-Lay workers in Topeka, educators were on the front lines, with nowhere else to go.

• • •

The unions had put out reasonable and rational plans to reopen schools as the pandemic allowed. The pandemic, though, was not a great time for the reasonable and rational.

In the fall of 2020, an economist named Emily Oster came forward with a provocative hypothesis, seemingly based on unassailable data: It was fine for schools to reopen. Kids wouldn't get sick, they wouldn't transmit COVID to their parents in any great numbers, it was all good. Music to middle-class parents' ears.

Oster wasn't a biologist or an epidemiologist. She'd never researched disease transmission inside or outside schools. Her biggest "contribution" to the data was a wholly unrepresentative sample of fewer than 1 percent of all school districts in the country self-reporting their data, from which she drew the sweeping conclusion that schools were safe to reopen; this was before even the first vaccines were available.[3]

Oster immediately found a following and was soon broadcasting her message all over the country in interviews and op-eds. She found a receptive audience in parents who wanted their kids sent back to school. Those parents, by astonishing coincidence, were overwhelmingly white; a poll in early 2021 showed that only 25 percent of white parents were concerned about schools opening too quickly, while a full 55 percent of Black parents were,[4] though the proponents of school reopening were quick to claim their real interest was the education of minority students.

Oster and her allies quickly constructed a false dichotomy: The teachers' unions and other left-wing fools, they claimed, were pushing to keep schools closed until there were zero new COVID cases. No one was saying that, but, as is so often the case, the unions' sensible and nuanced views were caricatured and ignored.

Randi Weingarten became the lightning rod for criticism. Despite her patiently explaining, time and again, her union's well-thought-out plans for reopening and evidence-based criteria, the narrative took hold: *Those selfish teachers' unions want to get paid to sit at home while kids learn nothing.*[5]

There are times (oh-so-many times, let me assure you) when unions can and do behave in foolish ways and embarrass the movement. For all the controversy over "learning loss" and the reopening of schools, this was not one of those times. Rather, it came at the end of a decade of near-incessant attacks on teachers' unions by the Right, and a decade of revitalization and renewal by the unions themselves, and it was unions' willingness to stand up and fight their own corner that sparked the backlash.

Education Unions, 2010–2020: Under Attack

Sixty years ago, when the labor movement was still riding high— when 35 percent of all workers were represented by a union, and politicians of both political parties bid for union endorsements— unions were overwhelmingly in the private sector.

There were unions in education, but they had very few legal rights to represent workers. The American Federation of Teachers began in Chicago in 1916 but operated more like a pressure group than a union. The National Education Association was for its first several decades a professional group that included (and was largely controlled by) school principals and superintendents.[6] There were moments of organizing and action—the first major strike by educators in the United States was by the St. Paul Federation of Teachers, in Minnesota, in 1946*—but union activity overall was low. The first state to pass a law giving public workers the right to unionize was Wisconsin, in 1959, almost twenty-five years after the NLRA.[7]

Public sector unionization accelerated in the 1960s. Among

---

* It's easy enough to find photos from this strike online. You'll notice, when you do, that the picket signs show two local numbers—Locals 28 and 43. An artifact of a different time: one was the men's local and the other was the women's.

other things, Walter Reuther, president of the United Auto Workers (itself brought into being by funds provided by the United Mine Workers in the 1930s), insured that the AFL-CIO provided significant funding for AFT organizing drives in major cities.[8] Organizing in the public sector was springing up everywhere. The Reverend Dr. Martin Luther King Jr. was assassinated in 1968 while he was in Memphis supporting striking public sanitation workers. Public-sector strikes became very common in the ensuing years, and in many states, legislators responded by passing laws giving public-sector workers collective bargaining rights.

Across the country, firefighters, public road crews, employees of state universities and community colleges, librarians, and other public employees unionized in droves, none more so than teachers and other public school employees. By the 1990s, union density (the percentage of an industry's workers in a union) was higher in the public sector than the private sector, but in terms of absolute numbers, most union members were still in the private sector because, of course, the private sector in the United States is much larger. By 2010, the numbers were almost even. The two teachers' unions, the AFT and the NEA, together account for around a quarter of all union members today.

This wasn't because the public-sector unions kept growing. It was because private-sector unions kept shrinking. The attacks on private-sector unions in the 1980s and 1990s had worked so well their numbers were dropping like a stone. As they got smaller, the Right's energy shifted more and more toward the public sector.

After the election of the nation's first Black president, Barack Obama, in 2008, billionaires like the Koch brothers, conservative think tanks like the Heritage Foundation, and Republican politicians went into overtime to attack progressive institutions and leaders. They coordinated their efforts through movements like the Tea Party (and later, MAGA), and policy groups like the American Legislative Exchange Council, which presented up-and-coming conservative state lawmakers with plug-and-play bills designed to dismantle public services and funnel more and more money to the very rich.

The attacks began in earnest in Wisconsin.

When Scott Walker ran for governor of Wisconsin in 2010 as a proud adherent of the Tea Party philosophy, he didn't promise to attack unions. He talked about reining in public employee benefits and pensions, but that had been standard Republican talk for years, in Wisconsin and across the country.

When he came into office, though, his first major move was Act 10; introduced on Valentine's Day 2011, it was titled the Budget Repair Bill, but the key elements of the bill weren't about the budget. It was an all-out attack on public-sector unions, the likes of which had never been seen before anywhere in the country.[9] The first state to set up collective bargaining for public employees was going to be the first state to watch that right crumble under a right-wing assault that had been planned for years.

In retrospect, the real surprise was how long it took before someone threw the punch. Union strength had been fading for decades. No longer did political leaders feel the need to kowtow to labor; even among liberal Democrats, unions were just one of many interest groups they needed to accommodate, and not necessarily the most important one. The continued existence of public-sector unions was a matter of inertia more than anything else. No one had tried to destroy them for so long that people seemed to think it just couldn't happen. But it could, and it did.

Act 10 was particularly clever in how it operated. The one thing it didn't do was take away public workers' theoretical right to unionize. By 2011, middle-of-the-road Americans accepted the right of public employees to organize. If Walker had tried to take that away, he would have looked very much the extremist he was.

Instead, Act 10 was death by a thousand cuts. Unions could still negotiate, but they could only negotiate wages, not benefits or hours or work rules, and they could only negotiate wages up to the rate of inflation. Unions retained the right to represent workers, but they had to prove that right by subjecting themselves to an election—every single year and at their own expense—that they had to win not just with a majority of votes cast, but with a majority of all eligible workers.

It was also death by confusion. Explaining all the insidious ways that Act 10 attacked unions took time. Walker and his lackeys could say, without outright falsehood, "Most public employees have the right to unionize here in Wisconsin. We just want to make sure it's done responsibly," and you'd need four paragraphs to refute them. National Democratic political leaders, who could have helped frame the issue more clearly, were largely silent. The unions were on their own.

Wisconsin set the pattern for attacks on public-sector employees, especially teachers' unions, over the next decade: be the devils who do damage in the details, and the public won't want to wade into the ins and outs of it all. Republican governors interfered with the rights of public-sector unions to collect dues and to negotiate over working conditions, but they kept paper-thin rights to organize on the books. The biggest blow was in 2018, when the Supreme Court issued its ruling in *Janus v. AFSCME.* Striking down a little-known precedent from forty years before, the Court gave all public-sector employees the right not to have to pay fees to support union activities, in effect making every state a "right-to-work" state with the stroke of a pen.[10]

The teachers' unions, however, had not been idle.

Education Unions, 2010–2020: Reform, Reinvention, Revitalization

In the 1980s, when corporations went wild on unions in manufacturing, mining, and transportation, their opposition was divided and weak. The AFL-CIO and the major industrial unions were not ready for the onslaught they faced. They didn't see it coming and couldn't figure out how to respond when it did.

The Right had the power to deal terrible blows to teachers' unions in the 2010s, but those unions weren't content to play defense. They found new ways forward that would serve them in good stead when COVID hit.

The American Federation of Teachers began in Chicago in 1916. In a nice bit of symmetry, the renaissance of teachers' unions also began in Chicago, in 2010.

That was the year when CORE—the Caucus of Rank-and-File Educators*—ran a slate of officers that won the leadership of the Chicago Teachers Union (CTU). CORE was founded by left-wing union leaders tired of stale CTU officers who seemed to have lost the will to fight. CORE's strength, however, wasn't just ideological: they knew how to build a union.[11] It's an important point to remember: Union reform isn't just about what you stand for; it's about knowing how to union and to union well.

Within two years of taking power, CORE led CTU on strike in 2012. It wasn't your typical strike, though. It was something new, something which we would come to call Bargaining for the Common Good, or BCG.

Nothing illustrates BCG better than one of the key demands of the 2012 strike, a demand they won. Here's the contract language. Maybe it seems pretty innocuous:

Teacher-editions of texts, instructional materials, curriculum guides for each subject area and supplies shall be available for distribution to teachers and an assigned classroom with a

---

* Taking their name, very consciously, from a previous CORE, the Congress of Racial Equality, a key organization in the civil rights movement, also founded in Chicago.

teacher desk on the first day of teacher attendance of the regular school year and the summer school session. Student texts shall be distributed no later than the end of the first week of student attendance.

Look at that last sentence. It doesn't have anything to do with teacher salaries, or benefits, or hours of work. *CTU went on strike so students would have textbooks the first week of class.*

It's long been common for educators, in K–12 at well as higher education, to say that "our working conditions are student's learning conditions." Such a remark was usually made when arguing for a wage increase: If you pay us more, we're going to be happier workers, less likely to leave and create turnover problems, and you'll attract better applicants for new jobs, and all of that will be good for students. Same with smaller class sizes—smaller class sizes help student outcomes but they also have a huge impact on teacher workloads. You can't help but notice the real focus is on the working conditions, not the learning conditions. There's nothing wrong with that—one of the reasons teachers unionized in such great numbers is that the jobs paid terribly and had horrible working conditions. But the slogan can feel a little self-serving.

But textbooks for students on the first week of class?

There's no financial benefit for teachers. It probably makes their jobs a little easier, to be sure, but the main beneficiary of this language isn't the teachers. It's the students. Think, also, about what's underlying such a demand; you wouldn't go on strike for this unless getting textbooks to students was a real problem. And, in Chicago, those students were likely to be Black or brown, and also likely to come from low-income families.

Textbooks for students, the first week of class . . . *in the contract,* in the legally binding agreement between the school district and its employees. They didn't just make speeches about it or confront the school board about the problem of textbooks. They went on strike. To get it in the contract. Using the tools of negotiating, for the common good.

In subsequent contract campaigns, CTU has pushed for affordable housing for poor students, improved transportation and on-site support services for students, and many, many more issues that you don't normally see inside a contract. The ideas of BCG spread across the country, becoming a core tenet of most union strategies by 2020.

Now, don't take this to mean that these unions don't care about things like wages. The huge #RedforEd strike wave in 2018, where teachers in conservative states like West Virginia, Oklahoma, and Arizona struck in droves, shutting down entire state education systems, were primarily strikes about pay. In those states, many teachers didn't even get close to a living wage.[12] While the wage gains in most of those states were fleeting, the experience surely reminded educators of the power of strikes; nothing makes workers bolder than walking off the job and living to tell the tale.

It's safe to say that, in teachers' unions today, you are less likely to hear "That's not something we can negotiate over" than at any point in time in the last seventy-five years, and you're less likely to hear "We can't go on strike" than at any time since the 1970s.

Which was perfect for when COVID came around.

Teachers' unions went into the pandemic ahead of unions in a lot of other places. They were already used to advocating for the whole workplace, not just wages and benefits, and educators were finding their muscle memory on strikes, too. This stood them in good stead when Emily Oster and company tried to bully school districts into reopening unsafely.

The Omicron variant hit in the winter of 2021–2022. Even vaccinated people were getting sick in large numbers. Fifty, sixty, even seventy employees a day at Eden McCauslin's school: "We were running out of adults." They had so few warm bodies that students were being herded into the auditorium and guarded by security, because there were no teachers to teach them and not enough people to watch teacher-less classrooms.

It was exactly the kind of situation in which it made sense to consider going back to remote learning. The kids weren't learning anything in the auditorium. They were being warehoused. This was happening all over the country. In January 2022, Philadelphia moved ninety-two schools to remote learning. In Texas, parents were asked to come in as substitutes. The auditorium solution was tried in New York, too.[13]

This needs to be stressed again because of how pervasive the antiunion narrative has become around schools. *When half the school's workforce is out sick, there is no good option. There are only the least-bad options.* Which was better: remote teaching, however imperfect it is, or having kids sit in the auditorium all day?

As Chicago Public Schools (CPS) dithered in January 2022, CTU decided to act. It wasn't a strike. Media reports then and now often call it a strike, but it wasn't, and that's important to remember. The union did not call for a work stoppage. Instead, they made a unilateral decision to switch to remote teaching until the surge in cases got under control.

CPS leadership had three options. The first would have been to support the educators and agree that remote learning was the best of a bad set of choices. The second would have been to have ordered the teachers back to school and taken disciplinary action against those who didn't return. An escalation, to be sure, but if your goal really was to preserve in-person schooling, it seems like that would have been the thing to do. If you were of the opinion that schools needed to stay open, stay in-person, then you'd order your people to come in in person.

CPS didn't do either of those things. Instead, they abruptly cancelled school, effectively locking out educators.* The union didn't want to cancel school. It wanted to switch to remote learning until case numbers got back under control. The bosses, though, couldn't tolerate the idea of the union making that decision on its own, and, as happens so often, their desire to punish the workers took precedence over the needs of the students.

After about a week, the union and the district reached a deal. They agreed upon an increased testing regimen, and metrics that would determine when a school district would switch to remote learning.

To put it another way, they agreed to exactly what the AFT had called for a year earlier—a sensible balance, guided by data, to get the best possible outcomes in a tough situation.

Striking for Justice

Again and again, educators discovered in 2022 and 2023 that school districts weren't going to do the right thing on their own initiative. The union would have to force the issue. In Chicago, it was around COVID safety, but educators took action for other reasons, too, including racial justice.

In March 2022, teachers and school support staff in Minneapolis went on strike for the first time in fifty years. The Minneapolis Federation of Teachers (MFT) had, in recent years, undergone a renaissance similar to the CTU and that of their metropolitan partner, the St. Paul Federation of Educators (SPFE).† SPFE had shown

---

* A lockout can be thought of as the opposite of a strike. Instead of the workers refusing to work, the employer refuses to let workers work, literally locking them out of the workplace.

† St. Paul, you'll recall, was the site of the nation's first major teacher strike in 1946. After the 2018 contract campaign, the union made the conscious choice to change its name from the St. Paul Federation of Teachers to the St. Paul Federation of Educators, giving equal voice to classroom assistants, special education aides, nurses, and other staff who made up the union's numbers.

its willingness to strike in 2018 (when members came within hours of walking out) and 2020 (when they did walk out), but MFT hadn't been ready in those years. In 2022, it was, and while money was certainly one of the reasons for the strike, MFT also struck for the remarkable purpose of compromising on a cherished union principle in the name of racial equity.[14]

LIFO means Last In, First Out. It describes how most unionized workplaces of all kinds handle layoffs: seniority. The longer you're there, the more security you have. The newer hires get laid off first.

There are good reasons for unions to support seniority in their contracts. Leaving layoff decisions in the hands of management means the bosses' favorites get picked, and the power to pick and choose who gets to keep their job is the power to divide workers and pit them against each other. Additionally, if the boss can lay off older workers, they can cut the highest-paid staff. So, unions want rules laid down in writing, not subject to the whim of a boss. Most opt, for perfectly sensible reasons, for seniority to be the determining factor.

But seniority has one significant drawback: In workplaces where layoffs are common, seniority rules keep new people from finding a home in the job, and when the new folks are different in some way from the veterans, those imbalances are then preserved by the seniority system. And because school districts face uneven funding from year to year, and student populations rise and fall, public education has lots of layoffs.

In education, therefore, this means seniority can be in conflict with the goal of building a racially diverse workforce, because seniority in effect bakes in the prejudices of a previous era. Like nearly every profession, Black and Brown people face barriers to entering teaching that white people do not, from outright racial discrimination in hiring, to more insidious and subtle forms of structural racism, to being more likely to be disciplined on the job, to having less access to family financial support to help them get through college and the first (poorly paid) years as a teacher.

Importantly, in a seniority system, these problems multiply each other; even if only a small number of people are affected by any one factor, the cumulative effect is that the teaching profession becomes disproportionately white, and that, in turn, means Black and Brown teachers are the first to be laid off.

Many education unions have dealt with this problem over the years by ignoring it. They just couldn't figure out a way forward. Sometimes, the union can't resolve the contradictions and fractures. When Boston Public Schools were faced with massive layoffs in 1981, for example, a judge (as part of an ongoing effort to desegregate the teaching workforce) ordered hundreds of white teachers with more seniority than Black teachers to be laid off, in violation of the contract, to maintain a racial balance.[15] If you had been in a Minneapolis Federation of Teachers meeting in 2010,* you would have heard the leadership strongly support preserving seniority, even if the consequence was that Black and Brown teachers would be shortchanged.

But the 2020 murder of George Floyd at the hands of Minneapolis police changed that way of thinking. MFT members saw how their students reacted with horror, outrage, and fear at such a blatant example of racist police violence, and most of them shared those feelings. Racial justice acquired the fierce urgency of now. MFT members looked around them and saw an overwhelmingly white teaching workforce. They also saw a school support staff workforce that was made up overwhelmingly of people of color with a starting salary of just $24,000. These union members also discovered the power of solidarity in the streets. Hundreds of MFT members participated in Black Lives Matter protests. In the schools, racial justice moved to the center of classroom discussions, with lessons informed by the personal experiences of students and teachers alike.

---

* As I was.

Negotiations broke down when the school district claimed there wasn't enough money, and so, on cold, ice-packed sidewalks, MFT members, joined by parents and community allies (including the author), marched in solidarity for three weeks.

Unlike private-sector strikes such as the one at Frito-Lay, it's rare for school districts to try to find replacements to cover for striking teachers. You need a license to teach, even as a strikebreaker, and there just aren't a ton of those folks around. Those that you can find were probably once members of the union themselves. So the schools get closed.

Because of that, success in school strikes depends on the members staying united. If they remain determined to stay on strike until their demands are met, they can win.

That's easier said than done, though. People need paychecks and health insurance, for one thing. But educators don't become educators to get rich. They become educators because they care about the kids. And as it is anytime you have a strike by people who do the job because they care about people (nurses are another big example), educators will stay on strike only if they're convinced it's better in the long run for those people, whether they be schoolkids or hospital patients. The strike quickly becomes a battle for the hearts and minds of parents. If parents show the teachers they support their strike, it makes it easier for them to stay on strike.

In Minneapolis, the parents overwhelmingly supported the strike.

The resulting contract gave substantial raises to school support staff, nearing their goal of a starting salary of $35,000. And the contract compromised on LIFO, requiring the district to protect educators in "underrepresented populations" from layoffs.[16]*

---

* While conservative critics have tried to frame this as favoring Black teachers over white, the language in the contract does not specify that particular racial or ethnic groups are protected. Theoretically, if at some point in the future white teachers are underrepresented in the district's teaching workforce, they would be the ones protected from layoffs while teachers of color with more seniority are let go.

It's always tricky for a union to take on contract issues that have the potential to favor one part of its membership at the expense of another. It's easier to stick with the current setup, even if that setup also favors some over others, rather than rock the boat and risk alienating members with a change. But MFT did it. The common good demanded that they prioritize racial justice in a city that desperately needed it, and that is what they did.

So Long, Detroit

Chicago and Minneapolis weren't the only places where education unions took direct action to fight for their students. In California, the United Teachers of Los Angeles (UTLA) walked out in sympathy with a separate union representing support staff, leading to the support staff winning a raise of *30* percent.[17] In Oakland, teachers' strike issues included better district support for students living in Section 8 housing and more accessible bus routes.[18]

If you needed more evidence that BCG was a winning strategy, there is no better proof than the election of one of the CTU staff who helped organize the 2012 strike, Brandon Johnson, as mayor of Chicago in 2023, defeating (in the kind of outstanding historical symmetry that makes it easier to write chapters like this) Paul Vallas, a former CEO of Chicago Public Schools.

Individually, the strikes (and lockouts) faced by educators in 2022 and 2023 showed that well-organized unions, willing to fight for what they believe in, can go far beyond just wages and benefits. They can fight for something bigger, and that's truly amazing.

Take a moment and go back to that piece of contract language I showed you earlier, about the textbooks. That little sentence is a direct assault on how contract negotiations in this country have gone for so long. It represents a better future for unions, especially in the public sector, to fight for more than themselves.

It's not about the textbooks themselves. It's about the

confidence and assertiveness of unions seeking to negotiate over things that unions generally do not contest. It's something unions had largely given up on for the past seventy-five years. Since the Treaty of Detroit.

It's 1950. The United Auto Workers is the most powerful union in the country. Its president, Walter Reuther, wants raises for his members, but he also wants something else: a guarantee that the car companies won't pass off those wage increases by raising the prices on the cars they sell. Reuther wants the workers' wage increases to come out of the company's profits, not the pockets of consumers.

Nothing was more horrifying to company owners. As has always been the case, employer opposition to unions is less about money than it is about *power*. About who decides.

General Motors wanted to be able to decide prices. Walter Reuther wanted the union and management to decide them together. He didn't get it. What he got instead has come down to us as the Treaty of Detroit.[19]

The UAW won, above all else, guaranteed wage increases, annually, above the cost of living. General Motors (and soon Ford and Chrysler, too) was agreeing to a contract that would raise living standards for autoworkers every year.

You know how politicians like to talk about "good manufacturing jobs" and how their policies will bring those jobs back? A hundred years ago, manufacturing jobs pretty much sucked. They were crazy dangerous. The pay was low. You got laid off a lot when the factory shut down due to seasonal demand shifts. The hours were long, it was hot, you didn't get treated very well. When you got too old or too hurt, you were out the door with nothing.

The reason politicians all extol good manufacturing jobs today isn't because manufacturing jobs are inherently good. They extol good manufacturing jobs because of the Treaty of Detroit. Because the UAW, and eventually the other big industrial unions, turned factory jobs into middle-class jobs, where a worker could support the family, buy a house, and retire at a reasonable age with a secure pension. Unions did that. The Treaty of Detroit did that.

But in return, Walter Reuther gave up the right to negotiate the price of the cars. It wasn't just that, either. With the Treaty of Detroit, the hopes of many union leaders—hopes that unions would go far beyond bread-and-butter issues and instead become full participants in all aspects of a company's operations—came to an end. It's not like there was a surrender ceremony or anything so dramatic, but after the Treaty of Detroit, unions found themselves limited to wages, hours, and terms and conditions of employment.

Unions continued to have lofty ambitions for a better world, and tried to make those visions real, but they did so through electoral politics, social movement support, public messaging. Not through the contract. The contract was where big ambitions came to die, buried by the treaty's troika of wages, hours, and terms and conditions of employment.

The teachers' unions, though, have pushed past that barrier. They've left the Treaty of Detroit behind. The era of BCG is one of nearly unlimited possibility for unions that are willing to take on the big fights. When they do, they win.

3

The Runway Not Taken

It's hard now, with unions nearly absent from whole swaths of the country, to imagine the breadth and depth of the impact unions had during the early 1950s.

Close to one in three American workers belonged to a union. In the private sector, unions were present in almost every major industry. Politicians of every stripe sought union endorsements, because the union vote was too big to ignore. Nearly all employers raised wages and benefits to keep up with unionized shops. Everyone knew someone in a union and almost everyone had a union member somewhere in their not-too-extended family. The minimum wage steadily rose. Taxes on the wealthy were high and stayed high. Inequality shrank as worker wages kept up with productivity for more than thirty years after World War II.

It was a period truly unlike any other in human history. Really. No working class has ever seen as widespread, sustained, and significant an increase in living standards as American workers saw in the three decades following the Treaty of Detroit.

We shouldn't romanticize it. The labor movement still struggled with racism, sexism, and xenophobia. Whole sectors of the economy, especially agriculture and domestic work, lived outside the protection of organized labor.* Unions, sometimes eagerly and sometimes

---

* These two things are connected to each other. The racism and sexism of unions did real damage to the movement by leading them to ignore certain industries that employed mostly women or Black and Brown workers. To take one notable

reluctantly, embraced anticommunism, and the American Left suffered, never again regaining the strength it had had during the 1930s.

But unions were strong. They had the ability to act in ways we can only dream of now. It's interesting to wonder how unions might have handled the crises of today if they still had the strength of yesterday. How might the strong labor movement of the 1950s have handled, say, COVID?

Perhaps we don't have to speculate. Perhaps we can look to places where union strength is still high, and where unions are able to use their strength to push for a better world. If we do, we can see the road not taken—a road where corporations needed to play ball with their workers every step of the way.

One of those places is the airline industry.

During the first two years of the pandemic, airline workers, specifically flight attendants, used the power of their unions to make sure their employers dealt with COVID very differently than those who employed Frito-Lay workers or schoolteachers. Right from the beginning, flight attendants exercised more power to protect their members than any other profession, and have used that power to launch an ambitious, huge new organizing drive in the most anti-union part of the country. There's much to learn.

Death at 30,000 Feet

Few situations seem less appealing, during a global pandemic caused by an airborne virus, then being cramped into a metal tube

---

example, unions missed out on the explosive growth of white-collar clerical jobs in industries like banking and high finance in the 1950s, 1960s, and 1970s, because so many of those jobs were held by women. The finance sector is the place in the U.S. economy where the real money is being made, and one wonders what might be different if unions had shown interest in organizing female-dominated occupations back when they had the resources and strength to do so. We'll see other examples throughout this book.

with 200 other people, 30,000 feet in the air. You're elbow-to-elbow, often with complete strangers, with no way to escape until you land.

If you think it was bad being a passenger at the beginning of the pandemic, imagine being someone whose job was to get into planes every day. Pilots, at least, have some minimal protection by being in a locked cockpit at the front of the plane, but the job of the flight attendant is to get up close and personal with—literally—every single other person on the plane. It just takes one of those people to ruin a flight attendant's day.

Of course, when COVID hit, a lot fewer of us wanted to fly. On a typical day in April 2019, there were 35,000 U.S. flights. In April 2020, it was 8,000.[1] Not many business models can survive a 75 percent drop in demand for any length of time. And workers don't have much of a chance of surviving a pay cut that size. People across the political spectrum agreed that federal intervention, in the form of a firehose of money being sprayed in all directions, would be necessary to keep airlines afloat.

But how would the workers fare in such a scenario? Would the dollars given to airline companies help workers, or would they go directly into the pockets of rich investors, leaving workers in the cold?

Airline employees had lived through this before, and seen "disaster capitalism" at its worst. In the wake of the terrorist attacks on September 11, 2001, the rich and powerful exploited the crisis to take money from the pockets of workers. Aviation unions' challenges after 9/11 were important preparation for COVID.

Sara Nelson, president of the Association of Flight Attendants (AFA-CWA, or AFA for short) and one of the most inspiring leaders in the labor movement today, remembers the atmosphere well. She was based out of Boston, working for United Airlines. The hijacked planes were on routes she worked. "I took suicide calls," from flight attendants despondent over the loss of close friends on the planes, she recalls. "We worked very hard at getting people home and checking on everyone and getting them help." Boston was a relatively small base; everyone knew each other. They relied on each other.

The response of the airlines themselves was . . . different. On September 12, the day after the attacks, when all flights were grounded, United got special government permission to fly one of their executives to Boston on an important mission. It was to tell the flight attendants that most of them should expect to be furloughed.

"There was this call across the country for patriotism," after 9/11, says Nelson.

> There were rounds of cuts, elimination of worker pensions, and a whole series of bankruptcies across the industry, followed by mergers that consolidated airlines and made them bigger. Congressional money flowed into the airlines after 9/11, but it didn't protect workers' pay. It didn't lead to lower fares. It kept executives and shareholders happy and not much else.

What makes the post-9/11 experience so frustrating is that the passenger aviation industry is one of the most heavily unionized in the country. If any group of workers could have successfully resisted the impulses of disaster capitalism, it would have been airline workers. In the post-9/11 atmosphere, though, with George W. Bush in the White House, even strong unions had to struggle to get a seat at the table, and usually it was the kids' table.

But the experience had an impact. It meant that when the next crisis rolled around, the airline unions would be ready.

Especially the flight attendants.

Solidarity at 30,000 Feet

The airline industry organized en masse in the 1940s, following the war. All the major airlines (save one) got unions of pilots, mechanics, ground crew, and gate agents. Flight attendants were in the mix, too, but as second-class members.

As soldiers and sailors demobilized and came home, hoping to return to the factories they'd worked at before the war, those factories obliged by unceremoniously kicking out the women who'd helped build the "arsenal of democracy," and for the most part unions acquiesced. Even those unions like the UAW that were committed in principle to equal pay and equal rights on the job for women struggled to practice what they preached. Union leaders by and large accepted the prevailing view of the time, that women were properly homemakers and that men should be the ones at work.[2]

The unions that organized airlines, though, were adherents of the "industrial union" philosophy trumpeted by the CIO in the 1930s and embraced by all of labor after the war. They organized the flight attendants, too, but placed them in the same union as the pilots, the Airline Pilots Association (ALPA). Pilots were paid much more. They had much greater status in the industry than flight attendants. And they were mostly men. While the early days of flight attendant unionism saw real gains—they won an eight-hour day in their very first contracts—the mostly female flight attendant union members struggled to get the same respect from the airlines as pilots did.

Sara Nelson recalls the words of a veteran flight attendant to her on her first week on the job. "Listen, management thinks of us as their wives or their mistresses," she told Nelson, "and either place, they hold us in contempt. Your only place of worth is with your fellow flying partners." The other flight attendants, she was told, might be the only people you can rely on.

Workers build solidarity and feel a sense of worth on the job, but the nature of the work makes a difference. Take Samuel Gompers, the first and longest-serving president of the American Federation of Labor, elected in 1886. He was a cigar maker, a highly skilled trade back in the days before machines did all the work. Cigar makers were a powerful force in nineteenth-century unionism, and while there are many reasons for that, one that stands out is the simple fact that they could talk to each other at work. Steel mills, railroads, coal mines . . . they're loud, and the work demands constant attention. You don't have time for chitchat. Rolling tobacco into cigars, on the other hand, is quiet work, so large numbers of cigar makers spent the whole day next to each other, and they talked. And when workers can talk, they can organize.

Flight attendants can talk, and they can organize. Planes are loud, and flight attendants spend much of a flight on the move, but they're near each other the whole time, on flights that last hours. They have to depend on each other to succeed. When Japan Airlines Flight 516 collided with another plane, caught fire, and crashed in 2023, it was the teamwork of the flight crew that helped ensure that everyone on the plane survived.[3] That kind of teamwork builds solidarity. Despite their subordinate status in the hierarchy of airlines, flight attendants built real power. In 1973, they left the pilots' union to form what became the AFA.[4] In 1977, the flight attendants at American Airlines, which had been part of a mechanics and ground workers union, split off to form the Association of Professional Flight Attendants. Their logo looks a lot like a Star Trek badge, which is pretty cool.

Over the years, the AFA and APFA have consistently punched above their weight, fighting successfully for the respect their members deserve. In particular, they developed innovative forms of militancy to fight and win. The most famous of these is AFA's CHAOS strategy, which also is the winner of the "union term that most sounds like a Bond villain's sinister criminal organization" contest. It stands for Create Havoc Around Our System.

CHAOS is best thought of as strike whack-a-mole. Striking is a powerful weapon, but it's also kind of a blunt instrument. Once you walk out, you're out; you've played your strongest card.

Striking is also high risk and high cost. Most unions provide some kind of strike pay for their members, and that can get expensive in a hurry. The United Food and Commercial Workers (UFCW) lost fully half its assets in the massive 2003–04 Southern California grocery strike and came away with not a lot to show for it; few think that strike was worth it.[5]

CHAOS is a way to strike without everyone going out and staying out. A flight can't take off without flight attendants; FAA rules prohibit it. So, in the 1990s, during a contract campaign for Alaska Airlines, AFA started launching strikes against individual flights. Just before a scheduled departure, the flight attendants scheduled for that flight would announce they were on strike. With no time to find a backup crew, and with federal regulations requiring flight attendants on planes, the flight had to be cancelled.

Alaska never knew which flights would be struck, or how many. Since most of its flights were still going as scheduled, and the flight attendants returned to work after each single-serving strike, it wasn't really possible for the airline to hire replacement workers, or to cancel flights in advance and rebook the passengers without so much fuss. Instead, whenever CHAOS struck, the airline would be left holding the bag, looking incompetent to its customers, but with no way to respond. It was devastatingly effective.[6]

Other labor leaders and activists took note of the power of CHAOS, and began thinking about how to adapt the tactic to their own work. In 2023, some of them ended up in key positions in the UAW.*

When COVID hit in 2020, Sara Nelson had been the AFA's

---

* AFA's CHAOS strikes are considered "intermittent strikes," and most American unions are prohibited from doing them, because they are considered illegal under the National Labor Relations Act and most public-sector labor laws. AFA could get away with it because airlines are covered under the Railway Labor Act, a different labor law that covers airlines and (you guessed it) railway workers. It therefore required a little creativity to translate the tactic to other industries. In the UAW, as we shall see, CHAOS became the Stand-Up Strike.

president for six years. She had risen to national prominence in 2019, when, with the federal government shut down in a political fight between President Trump and congressional Democrats, she gave a speech boldly calling for a workers' general strike to force the politicians to do their job. By astonishing coincidence, a few days after her speech, air traffic controllers began reporting themselves unfit for duty. It wasn't that many, just ten or so, but given the chronic understaffing of air traffic controller jobs, it led to (if you'll forgive me) chaos across the skies. Pressured by businesses who need a functioning air travel system to operate, Trump quickly caved and agreed to a deal to reopen the government.

Despite leading a union that represents only flight attendants, Nelson's vision is universal; she speaks of the working class in her public appearances, of the need for all workers, union and non-union, to unite in solidarity. Nearly all labor leaders invoke this kind of rhetoric now and again. The difference is that Sara Nelson really means it. That vision of solidarity was vital in the first days of the COVID emergency in the United States.

When she talks about that time, Nelson becomes visibly uncomfortable speaking in the first-person singular. Unions are run by members, and it's the power of those members, together, that allows them to do things. But, in the hectic early days of lockdowns and fear, Nelson was often the only person in the room representing airline workers. Maybe others would have done as well as she did—we can't know—but what we do know is that she came away with a better deal for airline workers than any other workers in the country got.[7]

On March 13, 2020, Friday the thirteenth, the day Trump declared a national emergency around COVID, Nelson was on her way back to DC from a cancelled meeting of the AFL-CIO Executive Council in Orlando. As soon as she got off the plane, she was on the phone to policy experts she knew from the recently ended presidential campaign of Elizabeth Warren. By that afternoon, she had sent an outline of a plan to Representative Peter DeFazio, chair of the House Transportation Committee. She outlined what she had recommended in a video she recorded for AFA members on the following Monday, March 16:

> We have told Congress that any stimulus funds for the aviation industry must come with strict rules that includes requiring employers across aviation to maintain pay and benefits for every worker, no taxpayer money for CEO bonuses, stock buybacks, or dividends, no breaking contracts through bankruptcy, and no federal funds for airlines that are fighting their workers' efforts to join a union.[8]

With only one really notable exception, that list became the Payroll Support Program (PSP) passed by Congress as part of the CARES Act on March 27. Within twenty-four hours of the pandemic emergency being declared, the AFA had laid out a bold vision for worker protection, and then they pushed it through.

The airlines resisted these proposals, as of course they would. They wanted the same free hand they'd had after 9/11—freedom to pass the money into shareholders' pockets while sticking it to the workers. Representative DeFazio told them he wouldn't pass anything without them talking to labor. Who should we talk to, the airline executives asked—Rich Trumka, the president of the AFL-CIO? No, said DeFazio; talk to Sara Nelson. And so, on Wednesday, March 18, Nelson sat down with a room full of airline CEOs and reached an agreement on PSP.

Other businesses across the country got the $800 billion Paycheck Protection Program, or PPP. Technically in the form of loans, most of which were forgiven, the PPP required recipients to "retain workers" but placed very few restrictions on how the money could be used. Analysts from the Federal Reserve Bank of St. Louis found that most of the money flowed to people in the the top 20 percent of incomes, and that a relatively small number of jobs were actually saved through the program.[9] More significantly, many companies took the PPP money and then used their own money (which otherwise they would have had to spend on the basic costs of running their business) for stock buybacks, executive bonuses, and large payouts to shareholders—exactly the way that airlines had used their post-9/11 bailout money.

The airlines didn't get that chance. The PSP strictly limited the airlines' capacity to take federal money with the left hand and pay out profits on the right. There were limits on stock buybacks and executive compensation, and on the ability of airlines receiving money to file for bankruptcy and break their union contracts. They were also prohibited from reducing the number of cities they served. Workers stayed on company payrolls and also kept their health insurance, thus reducing demand on state-run unemployment insurance and other social systems, and their paychecks kept coming even when there weren't many planes in the air, as did the taxes they paid to support public services.

"We had hoped that this would be a plan that would be used in every other industry," said Nelson, but it wasn't. Only aviation benefited, but not just the union members; while the AFA has only 50,000 members, the deal Nelson negotiated applied to all 2 million workers across the industry.* Consumers benefited, too. While prices across the whole economy increased 22.8 percent from March 2019 to March 2024, airline ticket prices went up just 2.6 percent.[10]

---

* This was also the case in Nevada, where the 60,000-member Culinary Workers Union represents nearly every worker on the Las Vegas Strip. In 2021, they got Nevada to pass a law guaranteeing every hospitality worker in the state—union and nonunion—the right to be recalled to former jobs as the economy opened back up. Most culinary workers already had those protections in their contracts, so the main impact of the bill was on the tens of thousands of Nevada workers not covered by the union. See Hamilton Nolan, "How the Mighty Culinary Union Survived the Apocalypse," *In These Times*, December 15, 2021, inthesetimes.com/article/vegas-culinary-union-pandemic-shutdown-workers.

There's no way around the conclusion. It was the strength of organized labor in airlines that protected them. Workers in industries with weaker unions didn't fare as well. Unions matter.

Anger at 30,000 Feet

Even during more normal times, flight attendants deal with a lot. My godmother was a flight attendant. In the 1960s, she was on a transatlantic flight. Soon after they reached cruising altitude, a passenger got up and went into the restroom for a long time. She emerged in a full-length nightgown, stood on her seat, and started climbing. The passenger thought the overhead luggage bins were beds, like the upper berths in sleeper trains, and that she could pull it down and climb in for a comfy rest. Flight attendants only wish their troubles were always so easy to laugh about.

By 2021, in no small part because of the Payroll Support Program, air travel had bounced back considerably; the existential threat to the industry was over. But it still meant being trapped in a metal tube with 200 strangers. A lot of those strangers were people who'd had their whole lives disrupted over the previous year, and who had, perhaps, lost some of the social skills that come from daily contact with people not in your immediate family. Tempers were running high, and flight attendants were in the line of fire.

"The violence was not over the masks," said Sara Nelson. "The violence usually broke out because they didn't have a place to put their bag, or someone put their seat back, or a flight attendant told them that they had to put their seat belt on." During the first eight months of 2021, more than 4,000 "unruly passenger incidents" were reported to the FAA.[11] On the more extreme end, a seemingly intoxicated Maxwell Berry punched a flight attendant and groped two others in the summer of 2021, leading the crew to tape him to his seat for the duration of the flight.[12] More common, and commonly unreported, were passengers swearing at flight attendants, refusing to follow crew instructions, and damaging airplane interiors.

Unless the situation is bad enough that taping the passenger down is an option, flight attendants really have no alternative but to stand there and take it. You can't (well, shouldn't) throw a passenger off a plane like you would throw a mean, ranting drunk out of a Wendy's. You don't have much available in the way of backup. And you have the constant risk that other passengers, even those who think they're trying to help, will escalate things beyond your ability to control them.

Airline unions rallied to protect their members. When a Southwest Airlines flight attendant was punched repeatedly by a passenger in May 2021, leaving three chipped teeth and landing the assailant fifteen months in prison, several airlines put a pause on in-flight alcohol sales.[13] Unions were concerned that alcohol not only fueled anger, but made passengers less likely to be compliant about wearing masks. Given that 3,500 flight attendants tested positive for COVID just during the first eleven months of the pandemic, mask-wearing was vital for their well-being.[14] Because airline travel is such a highly regulated industry, airline unions have long experience working with the FAA and other government entities to fight for the rules they need.

In retrospect, it's kind of amazing that an airborne pandemic didn't permanently decimate air travel. It wouldn't have been surprising if 2020 had led people to shift their travel and work patterns to avoid the confining atmosphere of air travel. Instead, air travel has bounced back, and despite the close quarters is considered a safe way to get from one place to another. The commitment of airline unions to the safety of their members and that of passengers is one of the main reasons why this is so.

The capacity of the AFA and other airline unions to organize and win big when the stakes are high is a key reason why they have the best shot of accomplishing what the American labor movement has tried and failed to do for more than a hundred years: building union power in the American South.

Organizing the South

When *nearly* all the airlines were unionized after World War II, there was one big exception: Atlanta-based Delta, the principal airline of the South. "[The union busters] never got lazy at Delta," said Sara Nelson. "They've been doing it since the forties." The new campaign led by the AFA, the International Association of Machinists (IAM), and the Teamsters, aims to organize the last of the big, legacy airlines, but it also has a larger purpose: to expand union power where its power is the weakest.

If you're wondering whether there might be a connection between the South's history—of slavery, treason in defense of slavery, segregation, lynching, racial violence, and efforts to prevent Black people from voting—and its status as the least-unionized part of the country, wonder no more. The desires of white Southerners to perpetuate white supremacy led directly to their efforts to quash unions, efforts which continue to this day.

As noted earlier, agricultural and domestic workers are excluded from federal labor laws. If you try, you can come up with arguments as to why those occupations *should* be treated differently than others, but it's a mistake to think any of those reasons were why they were originally excluded. It was all about race. Robert Wagner, the senator from New York who introduced and carried the National Labor Relations Act in 1935, needed the support of the Southern senators who controlled key committees. The price for their votes was to exclude jobs predominantly held by Black workers in the region. From the beginning, those in power in the South wanted nothing to do with unions because they saw them as tools for Black empowerment and (equally scary) unity between the Black and white working class.

Of course, sadly, racism wasn't limited to the South. A common tactic to break up miners' strikes in the industrial Midwest, for example, was to bring in Black workers to replace the strikers; most of the time, white union members directed their fury at the Black replacements as much as at the company. But the South takes it to another level.

It's important, though, to remember that while "the South" is a convenient shorthand, there are millions of people in the South, of all skin colors, struggling daily for racial and economic justice. Don't write off the South because of the actions of its political and business leaders. But don't underestimate the power of those leaders, either.

When organized labor emerged from World War II as an incredibly powerful part of the U.S. political and economic landscape, its leaders understood that the long-term survival of the movement depended on organizing everywhere. The mere threat of moving jobs to nonunion parts of the country would limit labor's ability to fight for more. Unions turned to the South. The CIO hired 500 organizers and, in 1948, launched Operation Dixie, the first, biggest, and, sadly, last comprehensive attempt to build union power across the region.

I'll spare you the gory details: It was a complete failure, and the single biggest reason was the ability of Southern political and corporate leaders to use racism to divide workers.[15] Solidarity is a powerful force, one that binds people together, but sometimes it isn't enough. The white power structure in the South used every means at its disposal—from judicial injunctions to stop pickets, to late-night fire bombings of union offices—to stop unions in their tracks, and by and large it worked.

It's tough for labor to win in the South. There is no more frustrating example than the two-year strike of a thousand mine workers at Warrior Met Coal in Alabama from 2021 to 2023.[16] Judge after judge issued injunctions that limited the ability of the company workers to picket. Local political leaders and the news media turned a blind eye to the suffering of the miners' families. While the national labor movement said all the right things, they weren't able to bring the kind of pressure needed to help the strikers, and the higher-profile interventions of progressive politicians like Bernie Sanders just couldn't move the needle. The solidarity and bravery of the workers and their families is the stuff of legend, but it wasn't enough.

Today, the South has fewer adults working per capita, lower wages, greater child poverty, lower life expectancies, and a larger prison population than any other part of the country.[17] Racism and union busting are two of the key reasons.

When Sara Nelson was negotiating with airline executives over what would become the PSP, Delta had just one priority: "Not saving the airline, not saving their workers' jobs, but making sure there would be no further unions on their property." The only part of the PSP that was a significant change from AFA's initial proposal was that it didn't prevent federal funds from going to companies that fought union drives. That was Delta's contribution to the discussion. Good for them.

Efforts to organize Delta flight attendants have fallen victim to bad timing as well as active union busting. AFA got enough union cards to file for an election in early September 2001. Ballots for the vote went out, in the mail, from our nation's capital, at the very same time that "every night on the news they were saying, 'Don't open mail from DC, it might have anthrax in it.'"

This might have mattered less except for one quirk of the Railway Labor Act. At that time, the National Mediation Board, which administers the RLA, had a rule (later changed) that a majority of *all potential voters* had to vote in favor of the union. Ninety-eight percent of the votes cast in that election were for the AFA, but in the fear-soaked post-9/11 world, they didn't get a majority of all *potential* voters. Subsequent attempts in 2008 and 2010 also came agonizingly close but fell just short. The 2010 election was particularly heartbreaking, because it came on the heels of Delta's merger with Northwest Airlines. Northwest flight attendants were represented by AFA, but losing the 2010 election meant those workers lost the union protections they had had for decades. Parallel efforts by the International Association of Machinists (IAM) to organize ground crews and baggage handlers also came close to winning, but not close enough. Each time, Delta spent truckloads of money to fight off the union drive, drowning AFA and IAM in a torrent of propaganda and fearmongering.*

The AFA and IAM are both at it again, along with the Teamsters, who are organizing technicians. This time, it's different. "With three unions" organizing at once, says Nelson, "the company doesn't know where to shoot. Support for unions across the nation is completely changing the conversations we can have in Atlanta. Elected officials are expressing support for the first time ever! People want to be a part of taking on corporate greed and setting the agenda for their communities rather than counting on corporations to do that." Getting contact information for Delta flight attendants is challenging, because there's no master list that employees can access, but when they connect with one, Nelson says, they join the union 70 percent of the time.

Delta attempted to buy off employees with raises, with promises, and with threats, and they still might prevail.

But maybe, just maybe, this time is different.

The South has seen more than a few surprises in recent years, like union election wins in the auto industry and higher education.

---

* It's not at all uncommon for employers to spend more money to fend off a union drive than they would have had to spend if the workers won their union and bargained a contract with significant raises. Corporate opposition to unions isn't primarily about the money, whatever they say. As we saw in chapter 2, the crux of the 1950 Treaty of Detroit was the automakers trading huge increases in worker pay and benefits in return for keeping control over core managerial functions. It is, and always has been, about control, not money.

Most promising, however, is the legacy of the 2018–19 "Red for Ed" strikes by teachers across the South. With a few exceptions, education unions in the South do not have the right to negotiate contracts with school districts.* Union power is harder to build when you don't have the foundation of a contract upon which to stand. But in 2018 and 2019, unions of teachers in the South displayed a fire and a spirit that shows us there's a lot of potential for labor power in the region.[18]

It started in West Virginia, where the primary issue was and is pay. (Even during the 2023–24 school year, five years after the strike, a teacher in many counties of the state with a PhD and *thirty-five years* of service made just $68,577.)[19] In 2018, the state was bleeding teachers; many left to find higher pay elsewhere, and many more quit the profession to find jobs that paid better. In addition, like flight attendants, the majority of the education workforce is female, and is subject to the same kinds of sexism, paternalism, and condescension that Sara Nelson described.

The West Virginia teachers' strike was organized as all strikes are organized—workers talking to workers, one person at a time, where they work and in their communities—but it was planned and coordinated online, especially through private Facebook groups.[20] They were helped by the wink-and-nod support of many school district superintendents, who were happy to have any help they could get to push the state to increase funding for education. The state's actual educator unions, AFT West Virginia and the West Virginia Education Association, didn't lead the strike and spent most of their time playing catch-up.

---

* In every state, teachers (and all workers) have the right to create and join unions—that's basic freedom of association, a right upheld even in the most conservative of states. What's missing in most Southern states is the right to collective bargaining—for a school district to be obligated by law to negotiate with a union if the teachers choose to be represented by one. Indeed, in most Southern states, even if a school district *wanted* to negotiate with a union, they are forbidden from doing so.

In February 2018, West Virginia educators shut down every public school in the state to demand the legislature fund wage increases for teachers and support staff. When the unions negotiated what they thought was a good outcome and declared the strike over, the rank and file ignored them, stayed out on strike, and got a better deal after a total of thirteen days out.

It's a mistake to call the strike spontaneous, because it scratches out all the great organizing that was done by educators across the state, but it's absolutely fair to call it unexpected. No one in the labor movement, on January 1, 2018, had "statewide wildcat teacher strike in West Virginia" on their list of predictions for the year. And they certainly didn't have what happened next.

Tennessee. North Carolina. Oklahoma. South Carolina. Virginia. Georgia. Arizona (not in the South but with similar labor laws). The strikers quickly came to wear red to symbolize their militancy, so they're remembered as the Red for Ed strike wave.

Strike after strike. Not all of them were statewide. Few of them came close to thirteen days. But they were strikes. In states where striking was illegal for educators, they walked out anyway. Black, Brown, and white teachers together, in solidarity.

And the public supported them. The contrast from 2011, when Scott Walker eviscerated education unions (in a state with a strong labor movement and a deep history of organizing) and largely got away with it, is, if you'll forgive me, striking. The cause of the workers was so obviously correct that the usual constellation of right-wing antiunion forces failed to tarnish their image in the public. In the American South, that's unusual.

It's true that there's been less lasting change from those strikes then one might have hoped. The South's politics remain antiunion, and racial justice feels even further away, as the Supreme Court's rulings in recent years have given Southern states more freedom to discriminate. Those strikes, though amazing and powerful, were not enough to transform the region.

But they happened. And that matters.

Former British prime minister Harold MacMillan was speaking to a group of schoolchildren after he was out of office. A hand shot up and a young student asked him what politicians fear the most. "Events, dear boy," he said. "Events."

The *fact* of the 2018–19 Red for Ed strikes hasn't gone away. It is now imprinted in the cultural memory of millions across the South. Tens of thousands went on strike and lived to tell the tale, and they were cheered and supported when they did so.

And since 2019 a lot more has happened. The UAW won a union election in Chattanooga, Tennessee, a place where it had lost twice before. Higher-education employees at Duke University—the flagship university of the South—won a union election vote 1000–131. In Fort Valley, Georgia, workers at the Blue Bird bus corporation won 12 percent raises in their first union contract.

These events matter.

None of this means that the South has overcome its history of racism and union busting. It hasn't. None of this means that the South's political and business leaders aren't going to do all they can to crush unions whenever they get the chance. They will.

But every win is a little puff of wind in the sails of the Delta union drive. They are a living, real, concrete reminder that a better world is possible. That matters.

Part II:
The Children of 2008

Every two years, labor's radicals and dreamers meet in Chicago for the Labor Notes Conference.

Labor Notes bills itself as the troublemaking wing of the labor movement. Despite never having had more than about twenty employees in its forty-five years, Labor Notes puts out a monthly newspaper of labor news from actual journalists, produces books on organizing strategy, holds well-attended Troublemakers' Schools across the country, and put on a biennial conference that, in 2024, attracted more than 4,500 unionists from around the globe.

I've been going to Labor Notes on and off for twenty-five years. It's not the same conference now as it was then. The general zeitgeist is similar—Labor Notes attracts optimists who want to build a better labor movement, and who believe it can be done—but there's something different now. The tenor, the tone, the energy . . . it's not just the general change of the times; it's bigger than that.

No one encapsulated it better than two older women I passed at the 2022 conference walking out of a packed ballroom cheering for Bernie Sanders. One turned to the other, and, not in complaint but in awe, practically shouted, "They're all so young!"

• • •

When I first got involved in the labor movement in 1997, it was like showing up to a party after all the cool people had already left. The beer was warm, the pizza stale, and the remaining guests were mostly older white dudes who stood in the corner reminiscing about how much better the parties used to be.

The labor movement of the 1990s—at least, how it felt to me—was weighted down by its past. We followed the paths of our forebears, not because they were right but because they were what we had. Those who wanted to innovate found themselves trapped by the institutions and traditions they inherited.

In the 2020s, workers who joined unions started throwing their own parties, and they were pretty great. And they developed their own traditions and institutions, and they seem amazing, too.

In a movement this big and this diverse, there is always something new. There are always green shoots, always moments of hope and excitement. There are always younger workers stepping up *someplace* and doing *something* new.

But the 2020s have been different. The 2020s have seen younger workers come to the fore, and they've proved themselves up to the challenge, inspiring the rest of the movement not just with the energy and enthusiasm that youth always has, but with commitment, strategic savvy, and great skill.

The twin shocks of the civil rights movement and the Vietnam War turned younger Americans away from labor unions in the 1960s and 1970s. That's an oversimplification, but not too much of one.

Many unions and union leaders supported civil rights. The 1963 March on Washington, where Martin Luther King Jr. gave his most famous speech, was financially and logistically supported by two unions: the (largely Black) Brotherhood of Sleeping Car Porters, led by A. Phillip Randolph, and Walter Reuther's United Auto Workers. Too many unions, though, supported civil rights in theory but not in practice. Construction unions fought to maintain the right to pass jobs on to sons and nephews, keeping the unions white. Teachers' unions in the North and Midwest were all in favor of ending segregation of Southern schools, but grew far more reluctant to make changes in their own neck of the woods. While unions in the 1960s had a higher share of Black workers than the country as a whole, unions could have done a lot more, and younger workers, especially, resented it.

Vietnam was just as bad. The AFL-CIO, and most of the major international unions, were rabidly anticommunist, and saw Vietnam as a struggle against international totalitarianism. Younger workers, who were being drafted and sent to war, or who knew those who were, were far less sympathetic. Once again, you find the UAW's Walter Reuther in a different place, one of the few national labor leaders to speak out against American involvement in Vietnam, before he died in a plane crash in 1970.[1]

In 1965 or 1975, if you were a young person rebelling against The Establishment, the American labor movement was *part of* that Establishment. Its leaders were people of great influence, hobnobbing with political leaders from both parties, participating in the civic life of the elite.

You really have to stretch the term to call organized labor The Establishment anymore. No wonder; when younger workers turn against the status quo, they don't see Labor as one of the things against which they turn. Instead, when they look to take on the system, they are turning toward labor. No demographic supports unions more than younger Millennials and Generation Z, with nearly two-thirds supporting them.[2]

"We're the children of 2008," said Caleb Andrews, when I interviewed him about his efforts to win a union for graduate employees at Johns Hopkins University. "We saw the banks fail."[3]

When I was fifteen, the Berlin Wall came down. We'd all lived our lives under the shadow of nuclear war—we really believed one was going to happen in our lifetimes!—and the end of the Cold

War was a moment for celebration and relief. A genuinely good thing for the world. Even if you were on the Left, it kind of seemed like the capitalist system was working, and that was hard to shake.

But if you were born in 1989, when the wall collapsed, what did you see? When you were twelve, the Twin Towers came down, and the United States would be in Afghanistan until you were in your thirties. You graduated from high school just as the Great Recession hit, and people you knew lost their homes, and your job prospects went out the window. For every win, like the Supreme Court ruling in favor of marriage equality, there was a loss, like the *Dobbs* decision that stripped abortion rights from millions. You made it to your thirty-sixth birthday without the minimum wage going up since you were a teenager.

When Trump came along, younger Americans were the ones most likely to resist his nativism, xenophobia, and authoritarian instincts. When COVID hit, they saw a society unwilling to do what it took to protect its most vulnerable.

More so than any recent generation, the children of 2008 knew they were on their own. They couldn't wait for anyone to help them. They helped themselves.

4

Solidarity Takes Down the Whale

Buffalo was both the most unlikely and the most fitting spot for the Starbucks campaign to start.

Two hundred years ago, Buffalo was like California was in the 1980s and 1990s—the hip, trending place, where new technology and new ways of thinking mixed with rapid economic development to create an exciting cocktail of ideas and adventure. The technology was the Erie Canal, a wonder of its time, whose impact on the United States was not dissimilar to the growth of the information superhighway over the past thirty years. Buffalo and the rest of upstate New York began to be known as the "Burned-Over District," as rapid economic growth brought with it waves of new ideas, fads, and trends that swept through the region like wildfires. Northern abolitionism and the U.S. women's suffrage movement found their firmest roots in upstate New York; it's also where the Mormon Church began.[1]

That's not the Buffalo we usually think of now. Today, Buffalo serves as an exemplar of the decline in the American labor movement over the past fifty years. In the 1950s and 1960s, Buffalo was one of the great industrial cities of America's postwar heartland, like Pittsburgh, Detroit, Cleveland, and Milwaukee. Buffalo had almost 600,000 people in the 1950s, working in steel, railroads, and shipping. Boom times.

Now we call it part of the Rust Belt. Health care and social services are the biggest employers.[2] The population is less than half of what it was in its heyday. White flight moved middle-class neighborhoods to the suburbs, so the poverty rate in Buffalo is double what it used to be.[3]

Buffalo was the leading edge when the Erie Canal came through. It was a proud union powerhouse during the heyday of American manufacturing. It's just possible that the next great wave in American unionism will come through retail work, and, if it does, once again Buffalo will be where one of the great labor victories of the 2020s caught fire.

The Very Model of the Modern Neoliberal Corporation

Named after the first mate on the *Pequod* in *Moby Dick,* Starbucks is as much a behemoth as that titular marine mammal, but it aims to be hip, cool, and a great job for young workers. "Millennials are our future," a Starbucks senior manager told *Cosmopolitan* in 2015. "They are forward-looking, technologically savvy, and deeply vested in their desire for purpose and meaning in their work."[4] Few other businesses devoted more time and effort to portraying themselves as an ethical, easygoing company, a "quasi-public meeting place" modeled on northern Italian coffee shops.[5]

Somewhat darker, more concerning stories about the unpredictable and haphazard scheduling of shifts, the low pay, and the safety concerns didn't get the same attention.[6] Starbucks was especially celebrated by the center-left faction of the Democratic Party, which, ever since Bill Clinton won the White House in 1992, had been hoping against hope that ethical employers would, of their own volition, make up for the weakening of the social safety net Clinton had acceded to while in office.[7] If employers would just understand the wisdom of treating their workers well, the thinking went, there wouldn't be a need for the kinds of conflict and tension that unions bring to the table. The admiration of Starbucks by Democrats was so great that—the historical irony here is too immense to measure—Starbucks CEO Howard Schultz was reportedly Hillary Clinton's pick to be secretary of labor had she won the presidency in 2016.[8]

The reality, though, is that a boss is a boss.

This is especially true in retail, where competition is fierce and investors demand ever-greater profits. Small establishments can be even worse; if just one person calls in sick, or if the customer rush is just a little bit higher than expected, workers can be overwhelmed but risk getting fired if they try to do anything about it. At Starbucks, one of the most hated practices (conjuring echoes of Frito-Lay's suicide shifts) was "clopening," where the same worker had to close the store at night and then open it first thing the next morning, with only a handful of hours in between to, you know, sleep and stuff.

One of the seeming advantages—for employers—of small retail establishments is that they seem immune to union organizing. Employee turnover is a constant in these small places, so there's little time for workers to develop deep bonds. And, besides that, what union would be foolish enough to try to organize a small store like a Starbucks? What leverage would the union have to negotiate a contract, when the company could close the unionized store and not even notice the hit on their bottom line?

It's absolutely true: Trying to organize just one fast-food restaurant or gas station or coffee shop or drug store just isn't worth the effort.

But what if you organized all of them?

Spreading Like Wildfire

It wasn't planned out. In 2021 and 2022, lots of workers tried to organize their retail stores. There were efforts at Waffle Houses, REIs, Home Depots, and probably scores of other attempts that never went so far as to be noticed by the outside world. Most of these followed the route that so many retail organizing campaigns of the past had followed: an initial wave of enthusiasm, followed by vicious employer blowback, then the efforts folded up or faded away. This isn't to diminish the courage of the workers who have organized and fought; it's just that organizing is, above all else, really hard.

So when three Starbucks stores in Buffalo filed for union elections at the end of August 2021, there was little reason to think it meant much of anything.[9] Two more union petitions filed in September were withdrawn before the union election. In December, the three original stores held their elections. One won, one lost, and one was stuck in limbo for a month as contested ballots were resolved. That meant, at that moment, five stores had tried to unionize and only one had succeeded.

But then two more stores won in New York, two in Massachusetts, one in Arizona. New York and Massachusetts, sure, but Arizona? By the end of the year stores had also filed for elections in Washington, Tennessee, and Colorado. All of them won their elections, too.

These Starbucks workers had one advantage that most other retail workers don't: Starbucks owned all the stores. The prevailing model in retail, especially fast food, is franchising. An independent company opens a McDonald's or a Subway by purchasing the right to do so from the parent company. The independent owner—the franchisee—buys its equipment, décor, and food from the parent company, and has to follow the company's rules on pricing and promotions and so forth, but each franchisee is its own company.

If you want to unionize McDonald's, therefore, you're going to have to organize each franchisee independently. It adds layers of complication and confusion to the process, and slows things down. Also, while franchises can be quite profitable, none have the deep pockets of McDonald's itself.

If this franchise model feels like a corporate dodge created for the sole purpose of making it harder for employees to organize across a whole company, well, I hear you. Labor lawyers have long been making the case that, in a franchisor-franchisee situation like McDonald's, there's not just one employer; the two layers are a "joint employer," both bound to bargain with a union. Had the 2024 election gone the other way, there's every reason to think Kamala Harris's National Labor Relations Board would have taken up the question, but no dice.

Starbucks didn't have franchises. All of the stores were owned by the home office, so to speak. Workers could look at the unusual geographic spread of the initial union wins, and see that this could be done anywhere. It helped more Starbucks workers hear what was going on and get excited. Starbucks Workers United (SBWU), affiliated with Workers United, itself an affiliate of SEIU, was investing time and resources into the campaign. By the end of April 2022, fifty union elections had been held at Starbucks stores. Workers voted to unionize in forty-six of them. And the wave was just beginning. It's more than ten times that now.

Solidarity, we've always thought, is more difficult at a distance. The great, mythic union victories of the 1930s, like the Flint Sit-Down Strike of 1936–37, when the United Auto Workers beat General Motors and opened the door to organizing the auto industry, were won by workers who lived and worked alongside each other. You could find whole blocks of homes where every single one had a worker at the factory in it. On Saturday night they went to the same beer hall; on Sunday they worshipped in the same church. If they were part of one of the many ethnic immigrant enclaves in Northern cities—Italians, say, or Poles, or Czechs—they might have a newspaper in their home language, even as the younger generations spoke English without any accent.[10] The reinforced connections between home and work made it easier for workers to trust each other, to stand up with each other, to fight together.

But skeptics, and for some time I counted myself one of them, failed to realize that what we thought was a universal truth, wasn't.

There have always been examples of solidarity working at a distance, but we dismissed them as flukes or happy accidents. But distance means different things to different people. And for Millennials and Generation Z, who grew up in a digital age where people thousands of miles away were just as easy to connect with as people down the street, solidarity could cross the nation with ease.

The more of those folks you talk to, the more it becomes clear that the Occupy movement in 2011 was an inflection point. At the beginning, Occupy looked like a stunt, performative theater designed to make participants feel morally superior while accomplishing nothing. Alex Press "recoiled in embarrassment" at the "hippie bullshit" when she first looked at photos of Occupy NYC, but she went with a friend to the encampment in Boston, and stayed.[11] It changed her life; Press is now one of the nation's most incisive labor journalists.

Despite some of the ridiculous trappings, the folks involved in the Occupy encampments were highlighting a real issue. The Tea Party had just swept into power in the House of Representatives. President Obama's agenda for reform—never a particularly ambitious one, to be honest—was dead. The Great Recession had thrown millions out of work and cost millions more their homes, but the financial systems that kicked it all off were barely touched, and the economic recovery was slow and uneven.

Labor historian Gabriel Winant recalls discussing with others how the *experience* of Occupy—rather than the message or the wins or the losses—might affect a whole political generation as well as

the individual lessons it taught and the ways that it became embedded in the life histories of those who went through it. As in all intense social movement cycles, participants would find themselves doing things they would not have anticipated, alongside people they would not otherwise have known. They would change not the state but themselves, and then carry that change with them elsewhere.[12]

And it wasn't just Press and Winant. Occupy was the first major national mobilization against concentrated wealth since the 1999 World Trade Organization protests in Seattle ended in clouds of tear gas. There were hundreds of Occupy encampments, some were short-lived, some lasted longer, and for every person who attended one, scores more heard their stories, imbibed their spirit. And while the people in New York and the people in Boston and the people in Duluth didn't talk to each other face-to-face, by 2011 (unlike 1999) you could share social media posts, send digital photos instantly, and create text chats with activists from anywhere to share experiences.*

Maybe Occupy was a lot of hippie bullshit. Maybe it was kind of silly. But it was there. For people, especially younger Americans, facing the absolute certainty that their future prospects were going to be more tenuous than those of their parents, Occupy was the option on offer to challenge the status quo.

It's also significant that Occupy was a movement based in collective solidarity; its signature slogan, "We Are the 99%," was a cry for collaboration and cooperation and organizing.

When I was entering the American Left in the 1990s, the cool thing to do was to go off the grid. It's not a surprise that Gen Xers, raised in the Age of Reagan, would view withdrawing from consumer culture and the rat race as the ultimate act of rebellion. But for people raised in the shadow of the 2008 financial collapse, the multidecade disaster of the so-called War on Terror, and the everwidening gap between the ultrarich and the rest of us, individual

---

* Also, unlike in 1999, long-distance phone calls had effectively become as cheap as local calls. Because it wasn't about new technology like email or social media, the rise of free long distance just doesn't get the same attention, but it surely was just as—if not more—important.

solutions seemed inadequate. It was necessary to band together, and events far away from home would matter for them just as much as things they saw every day. Where Generation X promoted individual emancipation, the children of 2008 embraced solidarity as a core virtue.

That was true for Jasmine Leli. She started work at one of the Buffalo Starbucks just after the first union vote, but it wasn't until seven workers were fired from a Memphis store in February 2022 that she first began to think the union effort was something real.[13] If they were firing that many people, there must be something to this. Why would they fire people if they weren't scared of the union?

"Violate the Law Here"

Starbucks Workers United proudly followed the tradition of the Burned-Over District; their organizing swept across the country in waves. In the first two and a half years, more than 400 Starbucks, and more than 10,000 workers, organized unions.[14] The union won more than 80 percent of the union elections, and Starbucks workers staged walkouts across the country in their fight for union rights.

For two and a half years, though, that's all they had—union election wins and short-term strikes. They were no closer to a contract in January 2024 than they had been when the first election was won in 2021.

Why? Because Starbucks knew, like so many companies before it, that they could openly and willfully violate federal labor law without any great consequence.

Let's imagine that a manager calls a female employee into the office. "We're firing you," says the manager, "because you're a woman and we don't want to employ women here." Just for the sake of this hypothetical, assume the employer doesn't even pretend to have a reason—the employee is being fired because the employer is sexist and doesn't care who knows. That firing (or a firing based on race, or national origin, or religion) is a violation of the Civil Rights Act, and also likely a violation of similar state laws. The employer potentially faces punitive damages, civil penalties, even, theoretically, *imprisonment*. It's a big deal. It still happens, sadly, and the Supreme Court has made enforcing these laws harder, but the laws are there.

What if you fire someone for organizing a union? What if they've got you dead to rights?

Well, first, there's no lawsuit in civil court. It's an administrative law procedure, called an Unfair Labor Practice charge, or ULP. In the case of Starbucks, it would be filed with the National Labor Relations Board, or NLRB. There's no risk of prison time. Not even possible under the law. No punitive damages—you'd have to repay the employee lost wages and rehire that person, *but* if the worker got another job while the case was being decided, you're really only on the hook for the difference between what the employee would have made working for you versus at the other job. No civil penalties or fines to the government.

The closest thing you'd face in terms of punishment—I swear I'm not making this up—is that you'd have to put up a notice on the company bulletin board, assuring people of their right to organize a union. Horrors. And if you rehire and then fire that employee again the next day for organizing a union, there's no escalation of penalties.

And let's say your repeated firings don't work, and the employees vote to form a union. Legally, you have an obligation to negotiate in "good faith" with the union. What happens if you don't?

Another notice on the board.

This is the reality of American labor law.

In 1978, a management-side lawyer named Leonard Scott handwrote a memo to clients on how companies should respond to union drives. On the bottom of the first page, he jotted out a little timeline of a union campaign. Right before "Petition filed" in the timeline, he wrote, with a little arrow pointing to where it should go: *"Violate the law here."*[15]

Mob lawyers at least have the sense to use euphemisms to hide the terrible things they're saying. They tend not to take notes on criminal conspiracies. Not the bosses' labor lawyers. Violate the law here.

Starbucks took that lesson to heart. In the fall of 2022, it rolled out a slate of new benefits for employees, including the ability to get tipped via credit cards, but denied those benefits to the stores that had organized unions. More than 250 Starbucks workers were fired during their organizing drives.[16]

SBWU had filed 750 ULPs, and had won favorable rulings in scores of them, including concerning credit-card tips, but nothing was changing. The company was gambling that they could continue to flout the law more or less forever, and that there was nothing the union could do about it.

Winning a union election, or winning 400 of them, didn't guarantee anything as long as the bosses didn't mind ignoring labor law.

It began to seem like the Starbucks campaign was headed toward a dark end, where the company's intransigence would win out over workers' efforts. This had happened before, especially with big corporations. In 2000, for example, meat cutters at a single Walmart in Texas won a union election 7–3 to join the United Food and Commercial Workers (UFCW). It was just one win, but within days, Walmart announced it was closing its meat departments at 180 stores. They denied it was because of the union drive, but . . . I mean, come on.[17]

There was a contemporary example, too, one that must have been hanging over the heads of Starbucks workers. The first wave of SBWU election wins competed for news with an even more remarkable victory. On April 1, 2022, a group of Amazon employees at a huge warehouse on New York's Long Island, operating almost entirely on their own, unaffiliated with any union, won their union election. It was the largest win in a private-sector union election in years, all the more remarkable because it was a true do-it-yourself effort.[18]

It was a seismic event in labor circles. The leader of the newly christened Amazon Labor Union (ALU), Christian Smalls, became an instant celebrity among union folks, making bold claims that the ALU was hearing from workers in more warehouses across the country and was going to organize them all.

And, then . . . nothing happened. Amazon tried to get the election result overturned (alleging, among other things, that Smalls and others had bribed workers to vote yes with marijuana)* but the ALU fended off that attempt; however, they couldn't do anything more. Amazon didn't even make a pretense of trying to negotiate a contract with the union, and many union supporters lost their jobs for dubious reasons. The ALU filed ULP charges, did the things they were supposed to do, but Amazon wouldn't budge. ALU leaders began fighting with each other as frustration with the lack of progress turned inward.

For all the brilliance of the initial election win, the Amazon Labor Union wasn't able to capitalize on that success. It seemed destined to fade away as its original core of leaders left and enthusiasm for the union waned—a powerful example of how, even when workers want a union, companies seemingly have little trouble holding them off.

More than a few labor folk felt that the Starbucks campaign was heading in the same direction. Sure, they'd won 400 elections, but there are over 15,000 Starbucks stores across the country; 400

---

* Smalls is Black, and the campaign against the ALU did not hesitate to traffic in the worst kinds of racial stereotypes to discredit him.

was just a blip. The company kept firing workers, kept refusing to bargain. How long before that campaign fell apart?

And then something truly remarkable happened. The union won.

"I've Always Had Hope"

There's a term of art used by labor scholars called *perceived behavioral control*. Its meaning is really pretty simple: Do workers feel like they can change what's happening to them?[19] The antiunion tactics of employers, above all else, are designed to eliminate such feelings. Make the workers see that they are out of their depth, that the power of the boss is just too great, and they'll give up.

This is the reason why even patently absurd or ridiculous antiunion claims by bosses can still be so effective. It's not uncommon for union supporters, especially people involved in their first campaign, to think that the answer to lies and threats is sunshine and truth. Just show the workers that the boss is wrong, and they'll still support the union. Rebutting falsehoods matters, of course, but it won't win you a union campaign on its own. Because even if you can prove everything the boss says is a lie, and every action the boss takes is a violation of the law, the boss is still there, saying *Go ahead, prove us to be liars. We're still going to keep lying, keep threatening, every single day until you give up this union nonsense. Is that what you want? To come to work every morning and hear nothing but antiunion propaganda in your ear for eight hours? To see your colleagues fired for no good reason? To live in fear that you'll be next?*

It's not a surprise so many workers have backed down from that. It's just human.

In the face of all that, what sustained the Starbucks workers was their solidarity. More than sustained—solidarity brought them victory. The ability of Starbucks workers to connect, at a real, personal level, across hundreds of stores and thousands of miles, seems to have made the difference.

Online solidarity played a role in many union struggles during the 2020s.

Take strippers, for example.

The dancers at Star Garden, a North Hollywood strip club, had traditionally regarded each other as rivals as much as co-workers, competing with each other for customers. But during the pandemic, when Star Garden was closed, a group of them formed an online co-op, performing shows over the internet to earn money. By the time they came back to work in person, one of the dancers known as Reagan told me, they felt a sense of solidarity they'd never had before. It led straight into a union drive and a long but ultimately successful effort to organize.[20]

Organizing over the internet is also proving its worth for the Emergency Workplace Organizing Committee. Originally started during the pandemic to help workers fight for safe working conditions, EWOC has evolved into a collective effort to help workers win positive changes of all kinds on the job, including union recognition. Though it receives some funding from UE and the Democratic Socialists of America, EWOC is largely run by volunteers. Workers cold-call EWOC with all kinds of problems: they didn't get their paychecks, the boss is harassing workers, no one's gotten a raise, the healthcare is being cut . . . everything. Workers are paired with a volunteer organizer who hears their needs and helps them figure out a plan to win. In the vast majority of these cases, the worker and the organizer never meet. It's done over the phone and online meetings. Thousands of workers have been helped by EWOC, and the model is one that could be scaled up quickly if unions wanted to invest in it.[21]

Solidarity built online can work.

The workers from Starbucks who lost hope, says Jasmine Leli, didn't see the global picture, didn't see the possibility of connections with people you'll never meet.

"You get really good at Zoom," she told me, describing the national bargaining committees and other cross-country entities SBWU established to coordinate their efforts. SBWU treated every newly organized store as an integral part of the group. Everyone was involved in the decision making, an exercise in national solidarity rarely seen in the annals of organizing. Hundreds of Starbucks workers were meeting each other, regularly making friendships, sharing understandings, commiserating, learning, growing.

Hoping.

It's always tough to understand a union organizing campaign from the outside. Too much is hidden below the surface, not shared beyond the group, so those of us who aren't privy to the internal conversations are always left guessing. I mention this because, from the outside, what Jasmine and others have told me and others feels a little improbable. But it's real.

Anyone who's been an organizer has seen the fake version of this, the pat on the heads of the workers. The professional staff organizers, the ones who "know what they're doing," go through the motions of telling the workers that this is a member-run union, that the workers themselves are in charge, and that they, the staff, are just here to help. Then they make all the decisions behind the scenes and stage-manage big meetings of members to rubber-stamp those decisions, giving a patina of member democracy to cover their closed-door decisions. Pat the members on the head, make them think they're in charge, while us professionals make the hard decisions. I know this happens because I've done it.

But Starbucks Workers United didn't have just any professional organizers helping them out. Workers United's organizing director was Richard Bensinger, the organizer who had helped found the AFL-CIO Organizing Institute in 1989. The new deputy director, hired in 2022, was Daisy Pitkin, author of one the best memoirs ever written on the dilemmas of the organizing profession.[22] The professional staff of Workers United could tell this Starbucks campaign was something different. Again, I'm looking at this from the outside. But the professional organizers genuinely supported the Starbucks workers making the big decisions themselves. That's rare, and while we may never know all the ins and outs of those internal conversations, it was important.

When SBWU's particular concoction of ingredients—internet solidarity, a commitment to participatory democracy, a steady stream of new election wins coming every week—met Starbucks' by-the-book union busting campaign, something happened.

When physicist Ernest Rutherford discovered the atomic nucleus in 1911 by firing neutrons into the atom and seeing with great surprise how they rebounded, he likened it to firing an artillery shell at a tissue and the shell bouncing back. Starbucks targeted its antiunion shots at the scattered, inexperienced, young members of SBWU, and each shot bounced back. Solidarity, it turns out, is made of strong stuff.

When Howard Schultz went to Buffalo to plead with the workers not to unionize in November 2021, it was supposed to work—big boss shows the common touch, makes the workers feel special and at the same time reminds them of the vast power arrayed against the union—but it didn't. His deeply personal anecdotes about being raised in poverty, and about how people in Nazi concentration camps shared their blankets, alienated workers who couldn't grasp why a multibillionaire was telling them it was okay that they made poverty wages.[23]

When Starbucks began doling out benefits to nonunion stores, like adding credit-card tipping, it didn't cause SBWU members to wonder if they should abandon the union drive to gain those benefits. Instead, "What gave us hope was we saw that it was possible," said Leli. For years, Starbucks had told them that credit-card tipping was not something they could provide to workers. Now, with just a few dozen stores organized, suddenly it was possible. Why would Jasmine Leli, and the fast friends she was making online across the country, give up now, when it was clear Starbucks was on the run?

When Howard Schultz testified before a committee of the United States Senate in March 2023, it was popcorn viewing for SBWU members, who were amazed that Schultz had come in person and were delighted to see many of their personal nemeses—managers who'd harassed them, supervisors who'd tried to scare them off the union—squirm in the audience as committee members shellacked Schultz. When Schultz relinquished control of the company the next month, they gave each other virtual high fives and knew they'd made that happen.

And all throughout the weeks and months that followed, more and more stores organized. At times the pace seemed to slow, and we all wondered if maybe the momentum was wearing off, but the solidarity that Jasmine Leli felt with her SBWU comrades stayed strong. They hadn't won anything for themselves yet, but they had hope, and what was ignited in Buffalo was now burning brightly from coast to coast.

Napoleon said that victory comes to the side that perseveres one moment longer than the other side. And as SBWU members were celebrating more wins, and meeting nationally to plot their strategy, the corporate leaders of Starbucks were also meeting.

They looked around. A public reputation in tatters. Young, enthusiastic, telegenic workers organizing store after store, seemingly unfazed by all that was being done to stop them. Twenty-one stores filing for union elections in a single week in February 2024. A pro-labor president, whose National Labor Relations Board was ruling against the company on a regular basis.

It's a source of enduring disappointment to me that we'll never know exactly what happened next behind those corporate closed doors. Corporate America is not an invincible monolith, but it's still pretty good at keeping secrets. So we don't know what room they were in, who was there, what else they were discussing. We're denied that moment of high drama.

But we do know what happened next.

Somebody looked around the room, took a breath, and said, "Maybe we should cut a deal."

And so they did.

On February 27, 2024, Starbucks and SBWU announced a deal.[24] On paper, it didn't really look like much—more an agreement to talk than anything substantive—but that's how these things often appear in the moment. The agreement to end the Flint Sit-Down Strike in 1937 was little more than a page, amounting to a union recognition clause and a means for resolving disputes.

Like 1937, though, the meaning of this agreement was not in the words. What mattered was the fact of the agreement itself. The goal of union organizing, in its most immediate sense, is to get to a place where workers can negotiate as equals with management. That's what Starbucks Workers United won.

Success has a thousand fathers, so in the years to come we will hear lots of reasons why SBWU won the most important victory for retail organizing in decades. All of those reasons will surely be worth mentioning. But one has to stand out above all others: the solidarity.

The Starbucks workers at the first Buffalo store went thirty-one months from the time they won their election to that February 2024 agreement. In that intervening time Taylor Swift released four albums. NFTs entered public consciousness, took over the public consciousness, and all but disappeared. Inflation appeared, peaked, and largely resolved itself. The UK had three prime ministers. Russia invaded Ukraine and the war was two years old by the time the Starbucks agreement was reached.

It takes a certain something to stick out an organizing campaign for thirty-one months. Unions and bosses alike operate on the assumption that it's not possible. It's wholly outside their experience. It *doesn't* happen.

Oh, sure, maybe you can find a core group of dead-enders who will keep the dream alive, because their personal politics are so prounion. That happens, a lot.

But to keep growing? To keep adding *thousands* of new members, organizing with the same level of enthusiasm and energy two years into the fight, despite no concrete progress, plenty of active repression, and no reason to believe an American corporation would ever come to the table?

It has to have been the solidarity. An entire generation, let down by every so-called leader and every cherished institution it had ever met, seeks strength within itself, reaching out digital hands all over the country and finding the will and the imagination and the fire and the spirit and the courage to stick it out.

The story is still being written, but it's one of the most remarkable and unexpected victories by organized labor in my lifetime or yours.

5

Organizing the Ivy League

R endi Rogers was working the plan.

It was election day, April 11, 2023. The graduate employees of Dartmouth College were voting on whether the Graduate Organized Laborers of Dartmouth (GOLD-UE) was going to become their union.

While she never said it herself, the people around her did: Rendi was a, maybe *the,* key person in the founding of GOLD-UE at the New Hampshire Ivy League school. She was at the heart of the organizing, the strategizing, the planning. Everything.

She'd helped build it, from the first time she and some fellow workers had traveled to Philadelphia in the fall of 2021 to attend a workshop on organizing and decided to apply the lessons they'd learned. She had been working toward this moment alongside her fellow workers for years. And finally it was here. The vote. The chance to win formal, legal recognition.

There was so much riding on that vote. Which is why the plan for the day was so odd.

They needed to make sure half the union's supporters didn't vote.

In the past few years graduate employee unionism, which has been around for more than fifty years, has seen more growth than any other part of organized labor. And not just growth. Dominance. In election after election, graduate employee unions have piled up margins of victory so lopsided that even dictators holding sham elections don't win by as much.* Try 1860–179 at Yale; 1696–155 at the University of Chicago, the intellectual home of neoliberal economics; 1414 to just 28 at Boston University. In a free, fair, secret ballot election, 1414 yes, 28 no. This was quite possibly the biggest margin of victory ever seen in a large union election in this country. Ever. The number of people belonging to graduate employee unions has effectively doubled in the past five years.

And it's not just the numbers; it's *where* they're organizing. As recently as 2019, if you looked at graduate employee unions, you saw unions concentrated on the campuses of state universities in mostly blue states: Wisconsin, Michigan, Oregon, New Jersey, Massachusetts, New York, California, Illinois, and so on.

In the last few years—partly because of chance, partly because of politics, and largely because of the determination and skill of organizing workers—the scene has shifted to the private sector. Now the entire Ivy League, save only Princeton, has a graduate union, and more and more of the nation's premier universities across the country—Stanford, Duke, USC, Northwestern, Johns Hopkins, MIT—have joined the state universities.

Comprising just 1 percent of the total number of unionized workers in the country, graduate employee unions have accounted for one out of every ten large strikes in the past five years.[1] Their explosive growth and success have turned grad unions from an interesting sideshow to movement leaders with the power and energy to topple national union presidents and bring ancient universities to heel.

It's a true organizing wave. Why? Why now? Why so many elite universities?

A key factor here is the failure of supposedly liberal institutions

---

* I'm not joking. When Syrian dictator Bashar al-Assad held a sham election in 2021, an election *no one* pretended was anything other than an act of theater, he gave himself only 95.1 percent of the vote. That puts him more or less in the middle of the pack of the union elections we're talking about in this chapter.

to take care of their workers. The pandemic laid bare the reality that even at the most distinguished universities in the world, graduate employees were labor first and foremost, to be exploited as much as possible. Exposed to COVID in the workplace, hurt by toxic supervisors and sexual-predator bosses, and struggling to pay the rent, the patience of grad employees ended.

But it's wrong to think of this as some kind of random wave. To call it spontaneous, spur-of-the-moment organizing . . . well, it kind of feels like they were just lucky. Don't kid yourself. It takes thousands of conversations, one person at a time. Building leadership networks, identifying the key people in every corner of the campus, learning the issues of every academic department, every lab group. Speaking a dozen or more languages to talk to workers from every corner of the world. So. Much. Work. And so much winning.

"Playing Union"

Who are grad unionists? For many years, graduate employee unions were primarily thought of by unions as entry points for the organizing of the rest of higher education, with the top prize being unions of tenured faculty. Their organizing efforts were supported, to be sure, but there was always an air of condescension, paternalism. *Good for those kids, with their little union there.*

This was the grad labor movement I came up in, in the late 1990s and early 2000s. We only organized the University of Illinois because of generous financial support from the AFT and the Illinois Federation of Teachers, but you could tell the rest of the labor movement didn't take us too seriously.

In large part, that's because graduate employees fit neither our picture of the modern university nor our understanding of a typical worker. And yet they are. They are integral parts of the higher education labor machine, and their work is as real as anyone else's.

The old line is that the three real purposes of college were sex for the students, football for the alumni, and parking for the faculty. That reflects a common view of who's in a university—students and professors. But faculty—that is, professors with tenure or on the tenure track—aren't even close to the only academics within academic labor.

The undergraduate in today's American university is primarily taught by contingent labor, much of it part time, with little job security, poor wages, and ever-poorer career prospects. Many of them are adjunct faculty, who often have all the academic credentials of a tenured professor but are hired semester by semester, class by class. They're Road Scholars, spending their time shuttling between gigs at different schools, trying to cobble together enough income to stay afloat, and hoping against hope that they can land a tenure-track job someplace, anyplace, and have just a tiny amount of security.[2]

At community colleges and small four-year schools, adjunct faculty make up the bulk of the contingent academic labor force. But at universities that offer graduate degrees, much of that work is done by the people seeking those degrees. In return for a wage and (usually) remission of tuition, graduate students work their way through their degree programs.

The two most common jobs are teaching assistant (TA) and research assistant (RA), though within those categories there is nearly infinite variety, and the nomenclature is far from standard. The "assistant" label for TAs and RAs doesn't necessarily mean they assist anyone. Instead, it represents the place of grad employees on the lowest rung of the academic ladder. It's important to understand how rickety that ladder has become.

Though graduate assistants face many challenges as *students,* organizing them has not been about academics. It has always been about their *work* in higher education. Graduate employee unions are as focused on wages, hours, and terms and conditions of employment as unions of assembly-line workers, teachers, or Starbucks baristas. Their working conditions are students' learning conditions.

And those working conditions have gotten progressively worse. When I became an organizer, a mentor told me about his experience as a TA at Northwestern University in the early 1970s. For the first year, he didn't teach a thing. He watched and learned, shadowing professors in large lecture halls and small seminar rooms, attending special workshops designed to train the art of instruction. Then, for his second year, he taught, but never alone, every move watched and evaluated by faculty who saw their role as preparing him for the future. For this experience he got his tuition covered and a stipend more than sufficient to cover all his living expenses in an expensive Chicago suburb.

The "training" I received as a new TA in the late 1990s consisted of half a day in a large lecture hall, where the primary lesson imparted to us was that it wasn't, strictly speaking, against the rules to sleep with your students, but you should be careful about it. Before I knew it, I was responsible for a hundred students, with a single visit from a professor halfway through the semester the only opportunity for feedback. I got paid enough to rent a studio apartment but had to borrow money to cover my summer bills.

The changing working conditions of grad employees are part of the broader trends that are damaging American higher education.

When the Teaching Assistants Association (TAA) at the University of Wisconsin–Madison organized the first grad union in 1968, tuition at most colleges and universities was low enough to be paid for with a summer job. Between the benefits of the post-WWII GI Bill and generous state funding, public universities were expanding rapidly in size and reach, making a college education a reality for millions whose parents never dreamed of such an opportunity. Graduate students could enter a PhD program with reasonable confidence that once they completed their degree a tenure-track job awaited, where they would take their place in ivy-covered halls, free to undertake research and teach the next generation.

Today's graduate students face a radically different experience. Student debt continues to grow as the cost of higher education rises and government support falls. Tenure-track jobs are harder and harder to find. In a growing number of states, tenure has ceased to exist in any meaningful sense. In Florida, for example, Governor Ron DeSantis has effectively handed higher education over to right-wing ideologues, who have ended tenure as we know it and have openly promised to purge universities of those who don't share his ideological views.[3] Corporations use universities as publicly funded R&D labs, siphoning off the profits into private hands while state funding plummets. Academic fields that don't lead to corporate revenue, such as the humanities, social sciences, and education, face cuts and closure. And this doesn't even begin to count all the things that Donald Trump has tried to do to universities in the last few months.

No wonder we turned to unions.

Rendi Rogers's challenge wasn't with TAs or RAs but with fellows.

At most universities, graduate students receiving fellowships didn't have to work. A fellowship was free money, allowing grads to focus their full energies on their academic work without needing to find paying work.

At Dartmouth, though, over the years, more and more fellowships began to have teaching and research duties assigned to them. Still called fellows, by 2023 these grads were doing the same work as TAs or RAs. In functional, practical terms, the jobs were the same, but the titles were different.

GOLD-UE was confident that, if they voted, more than 90 percent of fellows would vote for the union. But Rendi Rogers and her fellow organizers had to make sure they wouldn't vote. If they voted, they could ruin the whole thing.

Why? The short answer is that American labor law is incredibly screwed up.

When Is a Worker Not a Worker?

The TAA was formed in Madison in 1968. Unions in Michigan, New Jersey, New York, and Oregon followed in the next few years.* A wave in the 1990s and early 2000s saw unions spring up in Massachusetts, California, Washington, and elsewhere, and by 2010 there were probably 50,000 workers in graduate employee unions.

Their unifying characteristic was that they were all at public colleges and universities. The private sector was, in 2010, entirely free of graduate unions, though that had not always been the case.

It's all about the law.

Most private-sector employees get their legal collective bargaining rights from the NLRB. In most cases, those rights are relatively straightforward, but there are many categories of employees whose legal rights change based on NLRB decisions. Like the Supreme Court, the NLRB is an intensely partisan body that pretends to be nonpartisan. When Republicans control the White House, NLRB decisions tend to weaken labor's rights; when the president is a Democrat, it's better for unions. Following these decisions is like watching a slow, multiyear tennis match, the ball bouncing back and forth every time a different party takes control.

Way back in 1974, the NLRB issued a ruling that research assistants in the Physics Department at Stanford University were

---

* This chapter would have been far more difficult without the incredible website of graduate and undergraduate student unions built and maintained by the Washington University Undergraduate and Graduate Workers Union. They had as close to a complete list of all grad unions as anyplace in the country, both public and private sector, and kept it updated regularly, a labor of love and solidarity. It was at *https://wugwu.org/resources/graduate-and-undergraduate-student-unions,* but sometime during the writing of this book it went offline. I hope one of them reads this footnote and brings it back.

"students, not employees," because "the payments to the RAs are in the nature of stipends or grants to permit them to pursue their advanced degrees."[4] That is to say, the board ruled that they were being paid to be students. Game 1 to the bosses.

It stayed that way until 1999, when the United Auto Workers (about which more later) helped organize a grad union at New York University. The Clinton-appointed NLRB ruled that grads weren't just being paid to be students: They were performing significant work for the university and were entitled to collective bargaining rights. Game 2 to the workers.

Private-sector graduate union organizing began in earnest across the country but was almost immediately put in jeopardy by the arrival of George W. Bush in the White House. In 2003, I traipsed through the snow to help turn out votes for Graduate Employees Together–University of Pennsylvania (GET-UP). We gathered the evening of the second and final day of voting to watch the NLRB staff gather up the ballots and store them in lockboxes, unseen and uncounted, pending a decision. In 2005, Game 3 went to the bosses as the NLRB reversed their 1999 decision, and the ballots from Penn, Brown, Tufts, and other campuses were never counted.

It unaccountably took the Obama NLRB until the eighth year of his presidency to win Game 4 and reverse the 2005 decision, and as a consequence very little took place before Donald Trump took office in 2017. Everyone expected the match game would go against the workers.

But then, something truly surprising happened: There was no Game 5. The dog did nothing in the nighttime. The Trump NLRB never got around to undoing the 2016 decision. When Biden took office in 2021, graduate employee at private universities not only had collective bargaining rights, they had a reasonable certainty they would have them for at least several more years.

• • •

Sasha Brietzke was a fellow at Dartmouth. She was a key member of the organizing committee, a sure yes vote, but the plan was for her not to vote.

You see, even though the Trump NLRB hadn't taken away the rights of grad employees to form unions, "fellows" as a job category were still normally excluded. And even if Dartmouth couldn't stop the grads from organizing, they had an equally powerful weapon available: time.

Step 1 in the corporate* antiunion playbook is to buy time. There are so many perfectly legal ways that an employer can slow down the process, hinder momentum, dampen enthusiasm. It's a particular challenge for grad unions because of turnover.

There are many workplaces with higher turnover rates overall than grad unions; even before the pandemic, Amazon was losing 3 percent of its employees each *week*.[5] But workplaces with very high turnover usually still have some number of veteran employees, people who have been there ten or even twenty years and provide a bedrock of institutional memory upon which a union can rely.

Grad employees have a much shorter shelf life. It's rare to find a grad employee who's been in their job more than five years, and most work only two or three. This means that delay is a more powerful weapon. If you are able to hold things off a couple of years, your odds are pretty good that the rabble-rousers who started the effort will have moved on.

Dartmouth's voter list submitted to the NLRB excluded the 54 percent of workers who were fellows. If those fellows showed up and cast ballots, Dartmouth would use its entirely legal right to challenge their right to vote. This would be handled just like challenged ballots in other elections: The employer's observer at the vote would object to a fellow's vote being counted, the fellow

---

* And make no mistake, Dartmouth is a corporation, and operated just like one during this organizing drive.

would be allowed to cast a vote, but the ballot (a "challenged ballot," in the jargon) would be sealed and set aside.

In a union election, challenged ballots aren't counted if they aren't determinative. If the union wins its election 60–40, and there are five challenged ballots, those ballots wouldn't have changed the outcome, so they would never be opened or counted. But when the number of challenged ballots exceeds the margin of victory or defeat, the NLRB election administrator then has to rule on those challenges. The ones that pass the challenge are counted.

As you might guess, the process for resolving those challenges can take time. In the case of fellows at Dartmouth, even if the university lost the challenges (which it would have), it could have appealed all the way to a full NLRB hearing (which it would have), which could have taken years to resolve.

GOLD-UE found out about Dartmouth's plan to challenge the fellows exactly one week prior to the election. Rendi was in her lab when she started getting urgent text messages. She and the rest of the core organizers rushed into an emergency meeting.

Challenges to fellows voting would tie up the election result for a long, long time, long enough that workers might lose heart and give up the effort. Rendi, Sasha, and the other leaders of GOLD-UE knew that at least 90 percent of fellows would vote for the union, but if they voted . . .

It didn't take long for the plan to emerge. They had to move quickly, contact the hundreds of fellows, and persuade them not to vote. They would rely upon other workers to vote on her behalf. "I think there was a culture of trust that really allowed us to pull this off," says Rendi. "It seems like a strange thing to ask someone."

Not voting had to have been especially hard for Sasha Brietzke, because her story is significant in another way. She was a victim of the "unregulated and toxic" work environment in grad school. There were many such victims. Grad unionists in the pandemic organized, above all other reasons, because their employers refused to keep them safe on the job.

Safety and Shelter

Above all else, what made the children of 2008 organize graduate employee unions was the manifest failure of universities to provide for their employees' most basic needs. They had to look after themselves.

Academia is all about status and hierarchy. At the top are tenured faculty. Graduate students are second from the bottom, above only undergraduates.

Status is also power, and academia is "very much a patronage system," says Margaret Czerwienski, who we'll meet in a moment. "We're entirely dependent on our advisors. They have complete control over our lives." Their letters of reference, their comments to colleagues, their calls and emails on your behalf will make or break you. So will their silence. Their on-campus politicking will determine whether you get access to research funds, their connections across academia will give you your best shot at a job once you finish your degree.

In any workplace, even one with ivy-covered walls, significant imbalances in power lead to abuses of power. In higher education that abuse frequently manifests itself in sexual exploitation and violence.

Too often, sexual relationships between a professor and someone over whom the professor has power are ignored by universities. In all-male spaces, they can be the subject of approving nods and winks. The presence of large numbers of young women in classrooms and on campus is seen as something close to a perk of the job. Academics know this, but it's rare to see universities make any serious efforts to protect undergraduate and graduate students from predatory professors.[6]

When I was in graduate school, if a professor made advances on a student, the most common response—on the rare occasions any action was taken at all—was just to warn off future students before they fell into the predator's orbit, which is sort of like blaming the victims before they were victimized.

But the children of 2008 responded to the world they'd been given differently: They organized.

When Amulya Mandava and Margaret Czerwienski tried to warn new students about the predatory behavior of a Harvard professor of anthropology and African American studies, John Comaroff, he threatened their future careers. When Lilia Kilburn accused him of sexual harassment, Harvard obtained the notes of Kilburn's psychotherapist and gave them directly to Comaroff for him to use in his defense.

"We did all the things that the 'good girl' is supposed to do," said Mandava, and nothing came of it. Harvard's internal investigation largely exonerated Comaroff. That's usually what happens—the professor denies wrongdoing, and the university's interest is to sweep things under the rug rather than do the deep digging a thorough inquiry requires. They throw up their hands, and, pretending to know nothing about the nature of power dynamics in the workplace, declare that since he says he didn't do it and there wasn't video evidence, there's just no way to know. "This institution," Czerwienski says, "cares a lot more about Comaroff's property rights than it does about our civil rights."

Forty years ago, things likely would have stopped there. Twenty years ago, there would probably have been a lawsuit—as there was in this case, too. But what wouldn't likely have happened even ten years ago happened at Harvard: The union stepped in. "Our focus," says Mandava, "became how do we stop the harm from happening and how do we make this not happen again."

Mandava, Czerwienski, and Kilburn were members and leaders in the Harvard Graduate Student Union (HGSU). The union didn't have (and still hasn't won) strong contract language to protect its members from sexual harassment and violence, but it was a place of connection. They talked to other members, heard other stories from around the campus, and realized the problem was wider and deeper than even they had realized.

It's worth pausing for a moment to think about this: Unions create opportunities for workers to talk to each other that otherwise wouldn't exist. Without HGSU, there was no way that all these members would have met each other, learned what was happening to them, and figured out a strategy to address issues. When a union contract doesn't address a need, the union has other options, the biggest one being collective action.

At the beginning of the fall 2022 semester, and again in spring 2023, HGSU and allies staged strikes and walkouts to protest Comaroff being assigned to teach classes where students would be under his power. Some of this strike action might have been of dubious legality, but worker power matters more than legal niceties. While Harvard wasn't willing to take serious action against Comaroff, they also weren't willing to try to penalize strikers.

The dangers posed to Harvard students by Comaroff reached a resolution of sorts when he retired in the summer of 2024.[7] For our purposes, though, what matters here is something seen across all of the universities that have organized unions: the institution failing to take care of its people.

Sasha Brietzke at Dartmouth had also experienced sexual harassment. For most RAs, their work is done in labs controlled by just a few faculty members. "Each lab is its own ecosystem, its own silo," says Brietzke. The head of a lab, known as the principal investigator (PI), makes sure all the lab employees know that keeping them happy is the "only way to get your degree." "People are aware of the hierarchical structures," says Brietzke, and "people are angry about it." Brietzke and eight others had filed a sexual harassment suit against Dartmouth before the pandemic; she got involved with the union drive right away. "It would have been really nice to have the support of a union to negotiate these workplace dynamics."*

"This is what happens when you don't have a union," said Noah Wexler, part of the organizing committee at the University of Minnesota, which won its election in 2023. "All of us can be suffering. . . . There'[re] issues of harassment, discrimination, and abuse, and the university has been spinning its wheels on this." At Princeton, Promise Li noted the "culture of precarity and fear." There has been no effective route to help "student workers [who] have a negative experience with advisers on campus."

Abusive supervision wasn't the only reason grad employees felt unsafe. COVID made things even worse. "It's just been this kind of squeeze across the nation," said Brietzke. It "laid the foundation for the working class to say, 'We just can't do this anymore.'" In the summer of 2020, RAs at Johns Hopkins were being called back into confined lab spaces. "So many people have been told they were essential," reflected Caleb Andrews, "but [were] treated very poorly" by a university renowned for its cutting-edge medical research. Campus leaders at Dartmouth were "cartoonishly out of touch," according to grad Logan Mann. When the university expanded its child care facility to meet the expanded needs brought on by the pandemic, grad employees were still not eligible to use it for their kids.

As inflation began eating into worker wages in 2021 and 2022, grad employee wages failed to keep pace. Dartmouth grads had to go forty or fifty miles away from campus to find affordable housing. "You just can't eat and pay rent here anymore," said Brietzke.

---

* Brietzke was echoing one of the most famous union members in the world, Meghan Markle, aka the Duchess of Sussex. Reflecting on her treatment by the Royal Family in an interview with Oprah Winfrey in 2021, she noted, "At my old job, there was a union and they would protect me." Her old union, of course, was the Screen Actors Guild, whose monumental strike in Hollywood we will cover in chapter 7.

What was bad for grad employees in general was almost always worse for international students. In STEM-related fields, perhaps 50 percent of graduate students are from other countries.[8] As in many other fields, international workers are tied to their employers by their visas. International grad students are generally prohibited from taking employment off-campus, so power imbalances matter all the more. International grads are also more likely to rely upon the university to provide them housing, so their employers are also their landlords.

At campus after campus, international grads tried to use the university's existing procedures, but, like those at Princeton, as Promise Li says, they "got shut down. . . . When workers self-organize, we have less power to fight. . . . Without a union, we don't have enough power to actually demand" needed changes.

For decades, universities had fought grad unionization efforts by sowing fear among international students. COVID made clear that that trick had run out of power. "Every time people go talk to the DGS [Director of Graduate Studies] or their department head," said Cal Mergendahl at the University of Minnesota, "there's nothing to be done. . . . We're at the point where nothing else has really worked." On campus after campus, international grad employees flocked to the union.

Who is the best organizer of workers? The boss. When employers can't keep workers safe, workers will find a way.

The Wave

Organizing a grad union is like organizing any other union—one person, one conversation at a time. These unions are being built in the same way that William Z. Foster advised in one of the America's first written organizing guides, *Organizing in the Steel Industry*, written in 1936: "Individual recruiting is the base of all immediate organizational work."

Foster also wrote that these conversations "should be organized, as far as possible, according to department." This is also how grad employees did it—lab group by lab group, academic department by department.

It was also done largely by the workers themselves, rather than by professional organizers paid by unions. The gold standard research work on union organizing, Kate Bronfenbrenner and Robert Hickey's *Blueprint for Change* report from 2003, recommended a ratio of one staff organizer for every hundred workers. For campaigns the size of grad employee units, that would mean dozens of staff.[9]

They didn't need them. At Johns Hopkins, they won their election 2053 to 67 with the help of just two professional organizers. At Dartmouth, they had part-time help from one organizer, but were on their own otherwise.

This was vital, because the unions supporting the organizing didn't have the resources to spare. The first grad unions in the country were organized under the aegis of the American Federation of Teachers (AFT), which has long had a presence in higher education. The AFT, however, hasn't really been a part of the recent organizing wave.

Instead, the bulk of the work has been done by three unions, the smallest of which is doing the most organizing. That is UE, the United Electrical, Radio, and Machine Workers, which had only 30,000 members at the start of the pandemic but has by now effectively doubled that number.

The seeming mismatch between the work that workers do and the names of the unions that seek to represent them is a source of much amusement to labor folk. The truth is, we're long past the point where the official name of a union tells you much about who it represents. While we all say we'd like to have a more rational system in which all workers in a single industry are organized by a single union, that's not what we have.

UE got its start in grad unions almost thirty years ago. The United Electrical, Radio, and Machine Workers of America used to be one of the giants of the labor movement, with more than half a million members in the 1940s. But in the Red Scare that targeted the labor movement in the aftermath of World War II, the UE became a prime target, as its leaders initially refused to sign the anti-Communist oaths required under the Taft-Hartley Act. Kicked out of the CIO, raided by other unions, UE shrank in numbers but retained its militant roots.

When grad workers at the University of Iowa were looking for a union to help them organize, local UE leaders who represented State of Iowa employees volunteered. They lost their first election but came back just a few years later to win a brutally close campaign; the leading members of the organizing committee all got tattoos to memorialize their win. UE's deep democratic culture and radical politics made them a good fit for grad unions. Workers at Stanford; Johns Hopkins; Dartmouth; the universities of Minnesota, Chicago, and New Mexico; MIT; and Cornell have organized with the UE, among many others. Grad employees are probably the majority of the membership of the UE now.

Grads are nowhere close to a majority of the second union supporting this wave, but their numbers may very well have proved decisive in that union's success. The United Auto Workers (UAW) has long had a presence outside plant production lines. Many museum workers in New York, for example, have long been part of the UAW. The UAW got its start working with grad unions in Massachusetts in the early 1990s, and supported the massive University of California system-wide campaign mentioned earlier in this chapter. It jumped headfirst into private-university organizing, and recent wins at Harvard, the University of Southern California, and elsewhere have been supported by the UAW.

It is quite possible that the UAW is a very different union

today because of graduate employee unions. In the knock-down, drag-out fight for the UAW presidency in 2023 (see more in chapter 8), challenger Shawn Fain prevailed by just 483 votes—50.2 to 49.8 percent—but in grad union locals he won huge. with a margin of 777 votes in California's Local 2865 alone. Without grad union locals, it is possible Fain might have lost, and the course of the past few years may have been very different.

Along with the Service Employees International Union (SEIU), which organized campaigns at Boston University, Duke, and elsewhere, the UE and UAW have gone all-in on grad unions, and grad employees have been delivering.

The scale of the wins has been epic. In 2003, grads at Yale University, trying to demonstrate their legitimacy in the face of an intransigent administration, organized their own unofficial secret-ballot election to maintain momentum. But despite being able to choose the time, place, and manner of the election, the list of eligible voters, and who got to count the votes, the union still lost, 694 to 651. In 2023, the grads won 1860 to 179, bringing closure to a campaign that had been going on for nearly thirty years.

Others didn't take that long. At Johns Hopkins, while the quiet, on-the-ground organizing had been in progress for more than a year, grads signed more than 1,600 union cards on their first day alone. At Minnesota they exceeded 1,700. At Stanford, *2,571 cards in a single day.*

Within industries, there are union tip-over points, when unions move from the fringes to the mainstream. A slow, fitful progress can turn into a flood overnight. It happened with K–12 schoolteachers in the 1970s and early 1980s. It happened with industrial workers in the 1930s and 1940s. It's happening with grad employees now.

Among other things, this means that within a few years, most of the recipients of master's degrees and PhDs from the nation's top universities will have had experience in a union. Those graduates not only end up in key positions at colleges and universities across the country, but they also find themselves recruited by top firms on Wall Street and in Silicon Valley.

How will workplaces like Facebook and Google change when most of their new employees—freshly minted PhDs in computer science from Stanford, Harvard, and Northwestern—have helped organize unions in their workplaces? How will JPMorgan Chase and Goldman Sachs be different when their economists and finance experts from the University of Chicago hold union cards? What will happen to Big Pharma when their new researchers come in having battled and beaten their bosses in previous jobs?

I sometimes think about the administrators at Dartmouth. They must have been laughing and laughing, imagining how their foolproof plan was going to work when they announced on April 4, 2023, that they would challenge every fellow's vote. *Who cares how many GOLD-UE members vote for the union? When we file our challenges against every single fellow who votes, we'll tie this thing up for years. The grads will see they've got no hope of outmaneuvering us. Their union backers won't be willing to spend the money to fight the endless appeals. We'll win. Mwah-ha-ha.*

I wonder what they thought when, just a day later, GOLD-UE announced its response: GOLD-UE was going to ask all the fellows not to vote. I assume that, for a minute at least, those administrators must have laughed even harder. *No way can they organize hundreds of people not to vote! It'll be chaos!*

It could have been. GOLD-UE didn't have a legal right to, say, stand outside the polling place and block people from voting. They had to convince the fellows to not vote, and they had just a few days to do it.

They did. Rendi Rogers, Sasha Brietzke, and all the rest made it look easy. They won the election 261 to 33, with only thirteen challenged ballots.

Imagine sitting down at the bargaining table with GOLD-UE after that. After the union literally tied one hand behind its back and still got 89 percent of the vote. Imagine how much power it had.

The administration surely trembled.

Part III:

New Strategies for a New World

When a crisis hits, it's tempting to hold on for dear life. But sometimes, the crisis gives you the opportunity to make changes you may never have been able to make before. As the world is turned upside down (however briefly), the barriers to change drop. Maybe they don't disappear completely, but change gets a little easier, a little less fraught. It becomes a little more possible to say, "It doesn't have to be this way," and try something new.

Unions strive for unity, engagement, and involvement. Everyone, on paper at least, wants to have a union full of fired-up and activated members, ready to charge the barricades in the name of solidarity.

On paper. The devil's really in the details. You see, if members get fired up and excited, their expectations will rise, and it's possible those expectations will rise too high for comfort. I've known union leaders and staff from all sectors of the movement who felt that a big part of what they had to do was calm workers down, dampen their enthusiasm, so that they wouldn't develop "unrealistic" dreams of what the union could accomplish.

This behavior frequently gives rise to criticisms of selling the workers out and betraying the movement. Ah, but a man's reach should exceed his grasp, wrote Robert Browning, or what's a heaven for? It's always better to aim high, to set ambitious, lofty, extravagant goals, and then work like hell to get them.

I admire that confidence and drive, and I never like the idea of telling members not to aim too high, but I also can see where the hope-dampeners are coming from.

Much of the last half century has, for the labor movement, sucked beyond the telling. Strikes have been broken in pieces, scattering the union and the workers to the four winds with nothing left to show for the effort.

Ronald Reagan set the tone for this in 1981. The Professional Air Traffic Controllers Organization (PATCO) struck, certain that they controlled the skies and were undefeatable. Reagan fired them. The union was comprehensively broken. They were utterly defeated.

The 1980s and 1990s saw monumental defeats, one after the other, that are seared into the memories of those who lived through them. Eastern Airlines. Hormel in Austin, Minnesota. The Arizona Copper strike. A.E. Staley in Decatur, Illinois. Old, established unions torn into pieces. Good union jobs turned into mediocre nonunion jobs with great speed.

And even when the union wasn't comprehensively destroyed, it was retreating. Pensions disappearing. Health insurance getting more expensive. Wages not keeping up with the cost of living. Jobs contracted out.

And so I can understand why many good labor leaders have, especially not in the private sector, tried to keep their members from getting too excited, too worked up, because the best they could hope for was to stay afloat for one contract more.

But it doesn't have to be this way.

Feeling the winds change in the pandemic and in the Biden economy, some unions set their sights higher, and, to the wonderment of all, *won*.

The three biggest of these wins are the subject of these final chapters: the Teamsters' brilliant new UPS contract; the breakthroughs in digital won by the Writers' Guild and the Screen Actors Guild–American Federation of Television and Radio Artists (SAG-AFTRA); and, perhaps most amazing of all, the revitalized UAW striking the Big Three automakers and cleaning their clocks.

Each of these fights was a continuation of a long fight, one that the unions hadn't been winning for some time.

Each of these fights involved—before taking on the boss—an internal reckoning, where union politics brought new leaders to the fore, or united a divided membership behind established leaders.

I worked years ago with a veteran labor hand named Lee Johansen. He'd sit down with locals to advise them on bargaining, and he'd always say the same thing: *If you always do what you've always done, you'll always get what you've always got.*

These unions decided not to do it as they'd always done it. Each used ambitious and novel strategies and tactics, in each case trying things they'd never tried before. And each of them *worked.*

6

The New Flints

The modern American labor movement was born inside Fisher Auto Body Plant No. 1 in Flint, Michigan, in the winter of 1936–37. It was there that the United Auto Workers began their famous Sit-Down Strike, shutting down General Motors and winning union recognition for the first time in the auto industry.

Flint wasn't the first sit-down strike and it wasn't the last, but it was the most important.

In a traditional strike, workers leave the factory and picket outside of it, trying to prevent replacement workers from getting in and finished products from getting out. Today, we tend to think of picket lines as symbolic measures but in the 1930s a picket line was a real physical barrier. Trucks would be blocked, scabs assaulted, and the companies would regularly call in the police, the National Guard, or hired goons from Pinkerton or other "detective" agencies to break up the picket lines with force.

The sit-down strike cut out the "leave the factory" part. The workers stayed inside, physically occupying the premises. They fortified themselves, using unfinished car parts—frames, doors, trunk lids—to barricade the entrances, meaning that they would require much more force to evict, and creating the risk that such an effort would result in damage to the machines (less easily replaceable than the workers, in the eyes of the corporations).

General Motors made a considerable effort to evict the strikers from Fisher Auto Body Plant No. 1 (and, as they were occupied in turn, Fisher No. 2, and, later, Chevrolet No. 4) with vigilante groups and other hired thugs. But they weren't able to count on the state to help them. Newly elected Michigan governor Frank Murphy, who had been backed by labor in his campaign, refused to send in troops to clear the plant. He ordered the National Guard to keep the peace instead.* Denied the ability to force the workers out, General Motors settled, and UAW won a signal victory that spurred organizing across the nation.[1]

There are lots of reasons why this particular strike succeeded where others had failed. The novelty of the sit-down tactic, the lack of intervention by Governor Murphy, and the courage of the workers are surely the most important, but there's one more. In 1936 and 1937, if you had to identify the single most important node in the American economy—the chokiest of choke points—you'd probably have picked the GM plant in Flint.

Good union organizing always looks for points of leverage—the places or moments or tactics through which relatively small union efforts achieve the greatest effect. Bosses have, and have always had, more money than unions. They can afford to resist for a long time. To win, we have to find the places where we can have the biggest impact.

Where is the Flint of the twenty-first century? A pretty strong argument can be made that it's in logistics.[2]

The global economy is a finely honed ecosystem of mammoth proportions. Products are made from raw materials gathered from

---

* For what it's worth, Frank Murphy is one of the most underappreciated politicians of the mid-twentieth century. By not sending the Guard in, he not only saved lives but also helped the strike succeed; a world where a Michigan governor sends in the troops is a world where no one remembers the failed Flint sit-down. But Murphy wasn't done. Appointed to the Supreme Court a few years later by FDR, Murphy was also probably the first Justice to use the word "racism" in an opinion, when he wrote dissents opposing the use of concentration camps for Japanese Americans during World War II and discrimination against Black railroad workers by their own unions. See Sidney Fine's trio of books on Frank Murphy for the full story.

across the world, at factories on every continent, and then shipped everywhere, in a seemingly seamless web of commerce.

The workers at many points in that process are horribly abused. The environmental consequences of globalized commerce are staggering and frightening. But it does what it's supposed to do: get middle-class Americans, and their counterparts in other wealthy nations, what they want when they want it at a low price.

You can go to the supermarket with complete confidence that everything you want to buy will be on the shelves. You can go to the Apple Store confident that you'll be able to buy a new phone and they will have one right there ready for you to take home that same afternoon. You can design a car on the automaker's website with all the features you want, and the odds are pretty good they will find one and get it to you within a couple of weeks.

Even if it isn't always quite that smooth, it's pretty close. The modern global supply chain means production is carefully aligned with demand, so what is made is just what is needed. No need to store unused products—you don't have them. The sweatshop in Southeast Asia began producing the blue jeans long before it occurred to you that you needed new ones, and on the day you decide to hit the Gap, those jeans are already on the shelf in a store staffed by a minimum-wage mall employee.

It's an exploitative and deeply amoral system, but you can't help but be impressed with how effective it is.

Well, was. Because a lot of the foregoing became far less true at COVID's peak. That's when everyone realized we were working without a net. The lean, mean, slick global supply chain had no redundancies, no backups. It's stayed less-than-seamless ever since.

It was clearest with cars. Suddenly, you couldn't buy a new car anymore. The chip factories (largely in China) were closed for the pandemic and that stalled the whole thing. New car sales practically stopped, and the prices on used cars shot through the roof as people took what they could get.[3] Similar supply chain disruptions rattled the whole economy and were one of the primary drivers of inflation.

Logistics. The gears of commerce ran smoothly for years, until suddenly they didn't.

Workers were paying attention. Workers in logistics sit on so many choke points in our economy that just a few of them can exercise enormous power. The suspiciously coincidental illnesses of air traffic controllers, for example, which broke the 2019 government shutdown, and which we touched on in chapter 3, was a labor action by logistics workers. Look around you, and you soon see how many such opportunities there are for a few workers to muck up the whole system.

The labor resurgence of the last few years has seen some of its greatest triumphs, and also its biggest setbacks, among logistics workers. At one end, rail workers struggled mightily but weren't able to change the fundamentals of their difficult jobs. At the other end, the revitalized Teamsters, under new political leadership for the first time this century, won massive gains in the biggest labor contract in the private sector while making some unusual political decisions. And, looming over it all, the biggest Flint of the 2020s: Amazon, where workers are working every angle, some successful, some not, to win good jobs and fair working conditions.

Working on the Railroad

Railroads have been sites of ferocious labor conflict from the very beginning. The nation's first really big strike of wage workers,[*] the first to extend beyond a single place, was the Great Railroad Strike

---

[*] The nation's first big strike was not by workers who earned wages. It was the general strike by enslaved Southerners during the Civil War. There is still a great resistance, even in the labor community, to call this a strike, because there was no union, no contract, no strike vote—but that's nonsense. Thousands of enslaved Americans walked off the job and broke the back of the Southern economy.

of 1877. Starting in West Virginia, the strike spread like wildfire up and down the rails, paralyzing the country for six weeks until it was broken up by the U.S. Army, sent in at the behest of railroad owners to put down the workers.[4]

Armed agents of the government shut down plenty of strikes in the nineteenth century, but most of the time it was done by state troopers or local police. Intervention by the federal government, which at the time was tiny compared to what we know today, was much rarer. But the Great Railroad Strike made clear that, because rail strikes could easily extend beyond the borders of a city or state, the federal government needed to play a role.

As workers in rail organized, the federal government responded. For the first forty years, it was with force and repression. The Pullman Strike of 1894, for example, started in the Pullman factory outside Chicago. It quickly turned into a rail strike thanks to the work of the newly formed American Railway Union, led by labor hero Eugene Debs.

ARU members refused to handle trains with Pullman cars, and the whole rail system ground to a halt. The ARU was an attempt to build a single union of railroad workers, who (then as now) were made up of many smaller unions representing different parts of the work. Right away, though, the ARU let racism shoot them in the foot, as they refused admission to Pullman porters, nearly all of whom were Black, meaning a key segment of the railroad workforce didn't join the strike.* Once again, the president called in the army, which broke the strike. Debs was sent to prison for defying a federal injunction and emerged a committed socialist, founding the Socialist Party of America and becoming the people's tribune for a quarter of a century.

---

* Those workers were eventually organized as the Brotherhood of Sleeping Car Porters, the nation's largest Black union for decades, whose leader, Asa Phillip Randolph, was one of the true giants of the civil rights movement.

During World War I, the government took control of the railroads out of military necessity and passed laws to mediate labor disputes so that there would be no rail strikes to stop war production. The result was a system that worked pretty well and was slightly less oppressive to workers than unchained capitalism. It led to the passage of the Railway Labor Act in 1926, the first federal law that allowed collective bargaining for private-sector workers.

The RLA is still around in amended form and has features that are . . . peculiar to it. The most notable of these is a prominent, direct role for the federal government. Unions can only (legally) strike if they jump through a tremendous number of hoops, and it's not uncommon for the government to take a very active role in RLA labor negotiations.

As such, the decision of Congress and President Biden to stop a potential rail strike by forcing a contract on both the rail companies and the unions isn't a huge departure from past practice, but it was nonetheless a surprise for a labor movement that had generally found Biden a strong ally.

The issue was time off, not unlike that for the Frito-Lay workers we discussed in chapter 1. Trains—freight trains, anyway, which are the bulk of the nation's rail traffic—don't operate according to long-term fixed schedules because you can't predict when freight is going to need to be moved. Ships don't dock at ports on predictable long-term schedules, so you never know when a train will be needed to take stuff from the port. Similarly, the weather means that the growing seasons of major crops vary, so who knows when the wheat harvest will need to get picked up from the grain silos?

This means that rail workers, when they aren't working, are on call.[5]

Most of us have never been on call, or at least not seriously on call. Lots of us have had jobs where there was a chance the phone would ring and you could be asked to come in, but the ask is usually just that—a request, not an order. If you don't answer the call, no problem. If you answer the call and say no, they understand.

Emergency services, medical professionals, rail workers—their "on call" is different. The nature of the work means there's never a moment when you are safe from the phone ringing or the text message beeping, and when it does ring or beep, you have to respond, and quickly, or you risk losing your job.

It means even when you're not working, your work is there, just out of sight, waiting to pounce when you least expect it. You can't go on vacation because you have to stay close to work. You can't go off the grid in a canoe or at a campground outside of cell phone range. You can't drink alcohol or let loose. When you go to your kid's clarinet concert, sneak out with your better half for a nice dinner at a fancy restaurant, or lie down to sleep, you keep your phone next to you, ringer turned up, and a part of you stays keyed up, expecting the call.

Because of the unexpected pace of the railroad game, rail workers are on call a *lot,* and the only way to get out of being on call is to take a day off. But rail workers at the beginning of 2022 had very few days off. To use a precious day off to clear your schedule *just in case* you're called in . . . well, just think about it.

Rail workers went into 2022 angry about their lack of time off, especially their lack of paid sick days. They had been in negotiations since 2019—not uncommon in RLA negotiations, but still a long time. A possible strike was set for the middle of September, when a deal was reached that included some additional unpaid time off but no paid sick days.

It wasn't enough for the members of several of the unions, who rejected the deal and prepared to strike.

It's rare for union members to reject contracts negotiated by their own leaders. While rejecting a contract is, to many labor folks, a brave gesture and a sign that workers are ready to fight, it sometimes means the members aren't fully appreciating the realities of the situation.

On one side of that coin, you have the 2018 West Virginia teachers' strike. The unions for the teachers reached a deal with the governor and state legislature, but the rank-and-file rejected it and stayed out on strike. It was only after that display of commitment that the state enacted a 5 percent statewide educator salary increase. Rejecting that deal was a good move by the teachers.

On the other side is the disastrous 1981 strike by the Professional Air Traffic Controllers Organization (PATCO). After endorsing Ronald Reagan in 1980, the union had high expectations that he would repay that endorsement with a good contract, and the deal the union reached with the Reagan administration was, in fact, pretty good. But the expectations of the members far exceeded what was negotiated, and the union talked itself into rejecting that agreement and striking for a better deal. But instead of agreeing to a better contract, Reagan fired them all, completely destroying the union and sending a message to bosses across the country that they should play tough with their own unions.[6]

There was also the case of the Hormel Foods plant in Austin, Minnesota. When the company slashed wages nationwide in the mid-1980s, the union went along with it, but the local in Austin refused, going out on strike. The workers fought bravely and hard for a long time, but the company broke them, many of them lost their jobs, and they ended up with an even worse situation than they would have gotten without the strike.[7]

What happened to the rail workers was something in between. Congress passed—and in December 2022 President Biden signed—a law forcing a contract on the rail workers, preventing a strike. That contract had some expansion of unpaid leave, but no paid sick days.

While many in the labor movement were ready to call Biden a lot of foul names, there were also some whispered sighs of relief.

A rail strike might have led to gains, but it might have led to even more serious federal intervention than forcing a contract would. The economic impact of a nationwide rail strike, at a time when inflation was rapidly increasing, might have made the strike deeply unpopular. Also, not all of the railroad unions were ready to strike, and possible internal divisions within the rail unions would have been bad.

The December law wasn't, in fact, the end of the negotiations, either. Rail unions and political allies like Bernie Sanders kept up the pressure, such that a majority of rail workers did win (a paltry number of) paid sick days by the summer of 2023.[8]

The 2022 rail standoff isn't easily categorizable as either a win or a loss for the rail unions. Having the government step in and shut down your strike threat isn't something to take pride in, but the government's intervention supports the basic thesis of this chapter—that the rail system is so vital to our economy that the government will go to great lengths to protect it. Like Flint, if you *could* shut down the railroads, you would impact everyone.

So would shutting down Amazon.

Amazon

My day job is at the Economic Policy Institute. Monday mornings we have the Week Ahead meeting, where we map out our public work for the, well, week ahead. That morning in late March 2022, our director of communications was going through items we might want to amplify on our social media. "There's a union election at Amazon on Long Island. Maybe we should post some messages of solidarity."

Smart Experienced Labor Guy Kamper opened his mouth. "They're going to lose."

"Really?"

"For sure. They're going to lose badly."

Someone should have bet me.

It's amazing when baristas win election after election at Starbucks locations across the country, but you can tell yourself there are special circumstances. When the workforce is small enough that they all know each other by name, when they hang out after work together, when on any given day they barely see the bosses who are trying to union-bust them, well, you can understand workers hanging together to vote in the union.

An Amazon warehouse is a horse of a different color. Built as long as multiple football fields, employing thousands of workers on shifts around the clock, with huge teams of supervisors and cameras and electronic monitors watching everything that's going on—Amazon warehouses were built for the kind of union busting that corporate America has perfected over the past fifty years.

Workers have been trying to organize at Amazon facilities for many years, because working at them, well, kind of sucks. In 2019, I went to a Prime Day strike at the Amazon fulfillment center in Shakopee, Minnesota.[9] The Twin Cities area has the country's largest population of Somali immigrants and their descendants, and the Shakopee facility employs many of them. They led the strike, as they had led the organizing in that plant for some years, supported by local unions and especially by the Awood Center, an East African workers group.

One of the speakers at the strike rally was Mohamed Hassan. Picture everyone's favorite uncle at the family picnic—a ready smile, quick with a quip or a joke. You knew what was coming even before the translator told us what he said. He might have been fifty, might have been eighty—you know the type. "I am old" was all he said when asked.

But our favorite uncle walked with a cane, a bit of a stoop. There are bone spurs on his wrists and elbows, and the way he holds his left arms seems a little off, like it would hurt him if he tried to straighten it out too fast. When your favorite uncle is lifting hundred-pound boxes, three a minute for an entire shift, day after day after week after month, his body will start to break down.

Warehouse work is dangerous in general, but Amazon is a special case. Its rate of workplace injuries is almost twice as high as it is at other companies' warehouses.[10] During the period around Prime Day 2019, when I was talking with Mohamed Hassan, forty-five out of every hundred Amazon warehouse workers sustained some kind of injury.[11] The Amazon empire is literally built on the blood of its workers.

Set aside the quaint story of Jeff Bezos starting Amazon thirty years ago in a garage; it doesn't matter anymore. Amazon is a behemoth, and its ongoing success is *because* it's a behemoth. The logistics network it has built up means it can get things to you faster and cheaper than almost anyone else. If you were to try to start an Amazon competitor—Nile, maybe, or Mississippi or Ganges—you'd never get out of your garage.

But that behemoth status is also an opportunity. Like all the businesses in the logistics world, it can't go anywhere. It needs its fulfillment centers, its drivers, its global purchasing and supply systems. One of the biggest threats bosses make when workers unionize is that they'll close the shop down and move it to another state, or overseas. Amazon can't do that with its logistics business. They're stuck.

As such, Amazon does all it can to discourage unions. Surveillance. Intimidation. Retaliation. The whole playbook that we've seen throughout this book.

Amazon takes in almost as much revenue in a week as the entire American labor movement collects in union dues in an entire year. You can't just expect to walk in and unionize the place, you and a bunch of your co-workers.

And yet, that's exactly what the Amazon Labor Union did. As we discussed in chapter 4, working every angle they could find, relying upon great leaders on key shifts who could connect with workers, they managed to win. I wasn't the only fool who didn't see it coming.

And, for a little while, it felt like there might be a moment. There was also a close vote, right at the same time, at the Amazon warehouse in Bessemer, Alabama. It was a do-over election ordered by the NLRB after a 2021 union loss was overturned due to blatant violations of labor law by Amazon.[12] The 2022 rerun election came down to challenged ballots, just as the Dartmouth graduate workers that we saw in chapter 5 feared. They were right to fear. That 2022 election is still in limbo as the ballot challenges remain unresolved.

Similarly, the Amazon Labor Union itself launched a number of organizing drives at other Amazon facilities. Could they repeat their success elsewhere? If they could, there would be no stopping them.

They couldn't.

And so, ALU's story, while inspiring, also shows the limits of what workers at a single facility can do. Amazon has over one hundred similar facilities in the country, plus untold numbers more of smaller operations.

If Amazon was going to get organized, it would need a union with resources, patience, and know-how to target not just one warehouse at a time but scores of them, and it would need a union with experience in bargaining big private-sector contracts in the logistics industry.

That union is almost certainly the union that the ALU chose to affiliate with in the spring of 2024: the Teamsters.

Yes, the Teamsters

If you're not as deeply immersed in the labor movement as a dedicated labor nerd like me, when you think of the Teamsters, your mind conjures images of Mafia dons and briefcases filled with cash. Scorsese's *The Irishman,* that sort of thing.

That's not what the Teamsters are. But yes, it's part of their history. Not the only part, and not the most important part. The Teamsters led the way in the historic Minneapolis general strike of 1934, for example, carrying along the rest of the city with them, changing the whole pattern of labor relations in what is now known as one of the most progressive states in the Midwest. The Teamsters' National Master Freight Agreements in the 1960s and 1970s transformed the working conditions of truckers and remain accomplishments to be celebrated. Today, the Teamsters are a powerful and successful union representing almost a million and a half workers.

But still, when people think about the Teamsters, that's not what they think about.

Labor folks hate talking about union corruption. We've got good reasons. The stereotype of the mobbed-up union boss is embedded in the country's cultural DNA and it never does us any good when it comes up.

So, let's talk about it.

Some unions have been corrupt. The most common kind of union corruption is the same kind of corruption you see all over the place—people taking money that doesn't belong to them. A union treasurer "borrows" $300 from the union's bank account to cover the mortgage that month, that sort of thing.

The kind of corruption that people think of when they think of union corruption is organized crime. Unions run by mobsters, putting their family members on the payroll for jobs they don't show up for, threatening honest, decent businessmen with unspeakable . . . you get the picture.

That story is true, but it's true in the way it's also true to say that Amazon is a bookseller—accurate, but in a way that leaves out the biggest part of the story. For union corruption, it's the role of business. The worst examples of union corruption have *always* included the active participation of company owners and managers. It's not union corruption—it's *union-corporate corruption,* and its victims are the workers.

It's one of the greatest cons corporate America has ever pulled—erasing its own role as co-conspirator in frauds perpetrated against working people.[13]

You may hear about building contracts that give "no-show" pretend jobs to corrupt union officials, for example. You don't hear about how that can only happen when the company conspires with those union officials to agree to the scam, and the companies do it because those corrupt union officials agree to lower worker wages in the contract.

You may see something about a union "shaking down" a business. You don't see anything about how businesses that pay protection to criminals do so to protect themselves from strikes and worker actions; again, the company and some corrupt union leaders teaming up to stick it to workers.

You read in the paper about union officials stealing from a union pension or training fund. You don't read about how most of those pension funds—known as "Taft-Hartley trusts" because of law stuff we're not going into here—*are run jointly by employers and the union.* The only way union officials can steal from the fund is if the employers are also stealing from it.

If that last one rings a bell, it's because of the embezzlement of training funds at Fiat Chrysler by leading officials of the United Auto Workers (UAW) that was uncovered in 2019. The collusion with Fiat Chrysler's chief labor negotiators—collusion that was necessary to making the thefts work—is mentioned far less often.[14]*

The most insidious impact of this false understanding of

---

* It's interesting to compare the fate of the two organizations. The UAW was put under intense federal investigation and ongoing oversight. Fiat Chrysler paid a fine, mutated into Stellantis after a merger in 2020, and never faced any serious scrutiny, despite brazen criminality by some of its top officials.

labor-management corruption is just what we have here: We start a section on the Teamsters but then have to spend a few hundred words on corruption first. That's a tremendous disservice to the hard work of Teamsters across the country.

And you've got to understand: A big part of the reason we have to spend time on this subject is because corporate America is very, very scared of unions like the Teamsters.

Lots of unions brag and swagger. None do it half as well as the Teamsters.

Twenty years ago I was on a picket line in Chicago with striking university workers. A huge semitrailer emblazoned with the Teamsters logo came down the street. When it got to the picket line, it stopped. Didn't give a damn if they backed up traffic. A bunch of Teamsters in awesome leather Teamsters jackets (it was, like, 80 degrees) got out, and the sides of the semitrailer folded down. It wasn't just a trailer, it was a mobile stage. Microphones, big loudspeakers, even lights set up to illuminate the stage at night or flash cool colors to keep us entertained. This wasn't a Teamsters strike. Officially, they didn't have anything to do with it. But there we were, taking part in an impromptu strike rally in the middle of the street on a semitrailer stage.

It was pretty cool. And it scares the bosses like little else does.

The Teamsters have long been a union divided. Its reform group, Teamsters for a Democratic Union (TDU), is the model for most union reform efforts. Sharing offices in Detroit for many years with the staff of the reform-minded Labor Notes, the TDU for decades has been criticizing the leadership for insufficient militancy, self-dealing, and undemocratic practices, and pushing for a more transparent, energetic, and confrontational union.

The TDU had a spark of success in the 1990s, when Ron Carey, not a TDU member but endorsed by them, won the presidency of the Teamsters in 1991. It was under Carey's leadership that the Teamsters launched the most important strike of the 1990s, the

August 1997 UPS strike, winning a huge victory that included the conversion of part-time jobs into full-time jobs, significant financial concessions, and more.

If you, like me, had just signed your first union card a year before, that strike seemed to herald a new future for labor. But it was just another false dawn. Carey was already mired in scandal; he'd broken (or sat by while others broke) labor laws preventing the use of union funds to support his 1996 reelection campaign. He was removed from office and the internal confusion took the wind out of the Teamsters' sails. Teamsters for a Democratic Union returned to the opposition, and the 1997 strike became just another in a long line of "what if" moments for labor during our long decades of decline.

By the 2020s, the Teamsters looked very little like the Teamsters of their heyday in the 1950s and 1960s. The deregulation of the trucking industry in the late 1970s weakened the union's position in trucking, and its membership numbers declined. Long-haul truckers (who are occupationally descended from people who carried freight in horse-driven wagons; wrangling the *teams* of horses on those wagons gave the job, and therefore the union, its name) are now less than 10 percent of the Teamsters' numbers.

The Win at UPS

If the Teamsters are going to be able to take on Amazon successfully, and there's a lot of "if" there, it will surely be because of their long experience dealing with the United Parcel Service (UPS), another national logistics company. It's the strongest card in their deck. They know the industry. They understand the kinds of work being done. How the Teamsters fare at UPS tells a lot about how they might handle Amazon. Based on what we've seen the past couple of years, we have reason for optimism.

The UPS/Teamsters contract covers more workers—some 340,000—than any other private-sector contract in the country.

By virtue of its size, and UPS's leading position in the industry, the contract has the potential to influence the working conditions of hundreds of thousands of workers not employed by UPS.

Despite the big wins in the 1997 strike, the same problems continued to plague UPS workers in the years that followed. The biggest one was around job tiers. Employees hired before a certain date were compensated by one set of standards, while those hired after that were treated differently, and worse. Health care, pensions, wages—all were different to UPS workers depending on which tier you were on. And, because the best tier had no new people joining its ranks, more and more UPS employees were getting the short end of the stick.

Now, to be clear, this arrangement wasn't an accident. Unions agree to multitier arrangements all the time. To be blunt, it's a way of mollifying your current members by making things worse for future members who haven't been hired yet. Sometimes it's the only way to get a deal at the bargaining table. And every union that has ever agreed to a lower tier for newer hires has vowed to bring them up to the same level as that of the veteran workers. It's just that few ever succeed.

In 2018, the Teamsters negotiated a contract with UPS that, far from rolling back tiers, created yet another tier. The reaction from the members shook the entire union. They voted down the deal—kind of. While a majority of votes were against ratifying the contract, the Teamsters constitution required two-thirds of the membership to vote no, and so the leadership of the union went ahead and announced that the contract had been ratified.*

---

* This is another example of how the word "corruption" gets attached to unions even when the term doesn't really apply. The Teamsters constitution did indeed have this provision. The union's officers were following the constitution in approving the contracts. It was, I think, a pretty dumb thing to have in your union constitution, precisely because a moment like this might happen, but it wasn't corrupt of the Teamster leaders to ratify the contract, though many people then and since said so.

Whether the angry reaction from UPS members impacted the thinking of Teamsters president James P. Hoffa (son of the other Hoffa) or not, he announced his retirement in 2020, shaking up the union's internal alliances. The TDU teamed up with a former TDU critic, Sean O'Brien, for a united ticket that easily won the 2021 Teamsters election.

The new leadership went into the UPS negotiations in 2023 ready to fight. Conditions were excellent—unemployment was low and dropping, UPS profits were high and growing. The company could afford to give the workers a good deal, even if it didn't want to.

And the Teamsters were united like they hadn't been in a long time.

The alliance between old-school Teamster Sean O'Brien and the radicals of the TDU brings to mind the CIO's use of Communist organizers in the 1930s. John L. Lewis, the head of the CIO, was definitely not a Communist, but he needed good organizers, and the Communist Party in the 1930s had a lot of well-trained organizers in its ranks. So Lewis hired them. There's a general consensus among historians that their presence made a real difference in the growth of the CIO in the second half of that decade, with labor normies and Left radicals teaming up to take on the bosses.

In a similar way, the TDU was sitting on a huge pool of organizing talent. Its leaders had been excluded from involvement in Teamsters organizing for years because, as the political opposition, they weren't given a lot of opportunities to pitch in. Now the TDU was part of the governing coalition, and all the know-how and strategic savvy the organization had been building for years was put to work to win the best possible contract for UPS workers.[15]

As locals around the country began holding practice pickets in the spring and summer of 2023, and UPS began adding up the costs of a possible strike, the company began to move. It agreed to end forced overtime. It agreed to start air conditioning the trucks. It made movement on tiers. It made more movement on tiers. It looked around and realized that everyone in the country with a commercial driver's license who wanted a job had a job, and that the company wasn't going to be able to find strikebreakers very easily.

And so the Teamsters won. Every worker got an immediate $2.75 an hour raise. The most notorious form of two-tier employment was eliminated. UPS pledged to create 7,500 full-time jobs, reducing the number of lower-paid part-time jobs. Mandatory six-day workweeks were ended.

Like any contract, it was far from perfect. Some tiers remained for certain kinds of jobs, and critics thought more could have been done to help part-timers. Some of the details remained a little fuzzy, giving UPS room to wriggle out of some agreements, or at least try to.[16]

But it was a *real win,* and in so winning, the Teamsters reminded labor folks how hard those wins have been to come by.

What It Means to Win for Real

For the past four decades, unions have largely redefined winning as *surviving.* Yes, we gave up fully paid family health insurance, but we stopped them from taking away single health insurance, so that's a win! We wanted to add more vacation days, and we got a promise from the bosses to think about it—that's a win! They wanted to cut our base pay from $15 an hour to $12, but we kept it at $13.50, so that's a win!

The archives of the St. Paul grocery workers' union can be found in the Minnesota Historical Society. In those archives, you can read about Tom Kohler, who went to work for a local grocery store right out of high school in 1966. He made $2.94 an hour in a part-time job because of his union contract. Adjusted for inflation, that's $29 now. No part-time grocery worker in Minnesota is making anywhere near $29 an hour today.

For years after the Treaty of Detroit, unions drove up living standards for the working class to levels never before seen. But since the 1980s, it's been a rearguard action, a fighting retreat.

Not every single contract negotiated by unions was a retreat. You always have cool wins here and there. Always. Through 2021 and 2022, at workplaces like Frito-Lay, or in the Minneapolis Public Schools, there were wins like that—real, substantive, honest-to-goodness improvements. Not just postponing defeat, but moving ahead.

But there was no way to be sure if these wins meant something bigger than themselves. There were enough local factors, things specific to each case, that made it possible to dismiss them as flukes or outliers.

But you can't call the largest private-sector contract in the country an outlier. The UPS contract is living, breathing proof that unions are capable of winning, and winning big, even after decades of getting our asses kicked from one end of the country to the other.

If you boil down the American labor movement to just seven words, they are "It doesn't have to be this way." It's our belief that a better world is possible. We can make things better; that's what drives us. For a long time, that belief has been hard to hold on to.

But when unions win, it reminds us all that things can be different.

Just days after the Teamsters settled at UPS, tens of thousands of actors with SAG-AFTRA went on strike. A few weeks after that, the United Auto Workers went on strike against the Big Three automakers. I have to wonder: If the Teamsters had come up short at UPS, would SAG-AFTRA and the UAW still have gone on strike? I think not.

Of course, the Teamsters have, since that historic contract win at UPS, proceeded to make the rest of those in the labor movement scratch their heads in befuddlement and dismay. Sean O'Brien publicly flirted with Trump, spoke at the Republican National Convention, and refused to endorse Kamala Harris despite her participation in the most prolabor presidential administration since FDR's. This has led many supporters of O'Brien to reconsider their views, and one wonders how the radical members of the Teamsters for a Democratic Union are handling all of this.

But the Teamsters are so much more than Sean O'Brien. They are the rank-and-file thousands who fought and won at UPS, and who inspired the big strikes that followed them. And that's where we turn next.

7

Somehow Striking Feels Good in a Place Like This

One of the best bits of barroom-trivia-level labor history is that the only president of a union to be elected president of the United States was Ronald Reagan. Reagan, who fired the air traffic controllers. Reagan, who ushered in the union-busting era of the 1980s. Reagan, who oversaw a massive increase in wealth inequality and whose policies ravaged the working class, was president of the Screen Actors Guild from 1947–52 and again in 1959–60 (SAG merged with the American Federation of Television and Radio Artists in 2012 to form SAG-AFTRA). James Garner, one of SAG's vice presidents in 1960, said that, as union president, Reagan "never had an original thought," but it's also true that Reagan was one of the main leaders of the combined strike of actors and writers in 1960.[1] It was the last time writers and actors went on strike together until 2023. The ironies are myriad.

It serves as a useful reminder, too, of three important things. The first is that Hollywood is, and long has been, a union town. The second is that Hollywood's unions, especially those of its actors, are often led by people we've actually heard of.

For the third, reflect on one of the key issues of that 1960 strike: residuals. Residuals are the payments actors and writers get when their TV show is rerun, or when their film returns to the big screen for an encore performance. Just as songwriters and book authors get royalties when someone plays their tune or buys their book, actors and writers get a (pretty small) piece of the pie when a work they had a hand in creating generates more money. Before 1960, it wasn't that way. Actors and writers were paid for the work they did, and that was it.

But the third thing about Hollywood, the biggest reason behind both the 1960 strike and the 2023 strike, was that Hollywood is constantly changing.

In 1960 it was television. Before TV, movies came and went from theaters and once gone might never be seen again. Unless a theater wanted to do a classic film night or a tribute to a famous star, movies before TV fell out of the public eye once their theatrical run was over. TV changed that. Now, TV stations could run movies that hadn't been in theaters in years and the studios made money from licensing the film. It was that stream of revenue that actors and writers struck for (and mostly won) in 1960.

As Hollywood evolved, the unions struggled to keep up, sometimes moving ahead, sometimes falling behind. There was a 1980 actors' strike as the emergence of the VCR once again created new money flows. Writers struck in 2007 over residuals from shows streamed on the internet. Neither strike was an outright victory for either side. There's never really been labor *peace* in Hollywood— just armistices before the next outbreak of hostilities, because the nature of the business is always changing, and every change creates another moment for conflict.

You and I are a big part of why there was a strike in 2023. When Netflix and Amazon Prime and Hulu and all the rest began putting thousands of hours of film and television on their streaming platforms, we ate it up. No more trudging to video stores (that entire business model collapsed in less than a decade). No more $6 fountain drinks at the movie theater. On our couch, with snacks of our choice. Watch anything we want. Pause it when we need to get a refill. You can do all twelve seasons of *Murder, She Wrote* in about two months, if you're diligent, even with a full-time job.

We love it, we really do.

And the bosses loved it, too, because they were making lots and lots of money, without having to cut actors and writers in on it.

Until the actors and writers fought back, in one of the biggest strikes of 2023.

The story of the strike has been told in many places. For our purposes, the part of the story that matters most is how the fractious and feuding Hollywood unions found a way forward to stand together. The strike is the strongest argument of recent years that solidarity matters more than anything else. When union members are at odds (not just between unions but within them), they lose. When they unite, they can win.

Divide and Conquer

The old line is that power comes in two forms: organized money and organized people. The bosses do the first, the workers do the second. As such, a basic strategic imperative for bosses, at any time and in any industry, is to keep workers from getting organized. In much of America today, you do that by preventing workers from unionizing in the first place. American labor law is so broken that companies like Starbucks generally think they can push back against strong worker organizing for years at little cost and even less risk. They're usually right. Usually.

If you want to see corporations do this very well, look at gig drivers. Uber, Lyft, DoorDash, and the other companies are often described as leading-edge, innovative firms revitalizing an industry. But what exactly are they innovating? They don't offer new services; we've been able to call for a taxi as long as there have been phones. They don't create new products; they're service businesses. They don't even utilize new technology, not really. They've created apps. High schoolers create apps.

The "innovation" of gig driver companies is that they have

figured out how to push all the real costs of the business onto their workers, who they then argue aren't even their workers. A taxicab company has to own all the taxis, fuel them, clean them, repair them. It has to pay its employees during slack periods and charge fares that are (in most places) heavily regulated by the city. If one of its drivers is in an accident, it can be sued.

Uber and Lyft got rid of all of that. Drivers own their own vehicles, and get paid only when they have a passenger. The liability is theirs, but the prices Uber and Lyft charge are arbitrary and subject to change on a whim. The worker assumes all the risk, and the company takes whatever share of the money it wants. It's evil, sure, but you gotta admit it's brilliant. When smart and persuasive arguments are made that this business model is plainly a violation of labor law, the companies throw money at lawyers, politicians, and media companies so that efforts to regulate them fall short.[2]

But they've also done a great job of dividing unions. In Washington, Massachusetts, and elsewhere, Uber and Lyft have persuaded some unions to cooperate with them, extending a patina of union recognition (but no real bargaining power) in return for those unions endorsing those business models. These decisions are hugely controversial in the labor movement, and the controversy itself is perhaps the gig companies' biggest win: The fighting between unions inhibits meaningful action.[3]

But there are industries or parts of the country where workers are already well organized, and where divide-and-conquer isn't as easy to pull off—outposts of labor strength where, despite the onslaught of the past half century, workers still wield real power. There are still a lot of these, even as labor's overall power is a fraction of what it once was.

Visit the Strip in Las Vegas, for example, to see this in practice. The Culinary Workers Union, UNITE-HERE Local 226, is a desert powerhouse. At the Mandalay Bay Resort or Caesar's Palace (or the Trump International Hotel Las Vegas, for that matter), you can get a job cleaning hotel rooms, graduate to dealing blackjack, then take a class offered through the union to become a chef. In all the jobs, you get health insurance, a good pension, and wages that usually start above $20 an hour.

Nevada is a right-to-work state. Unions are supposed to wither and die there. That's the whole reason to pass right-to-work laws. But the Culinary Workers sometimes use the University of Nevada, Las Vegas (UNLV) football stadium for their membership meetings because it's the only venue in town big enough to hold them all.[4] In 2024, they succeeded in organizing the last two holdouts on the Strip—the Venetian and the Palazzo. Now every single hotel is unionized, pretty much top to bottom.

You find these islands of power all over the place: Most of the country's major ports. The airline industry. Cleaning crews in downtown office buildings in lots of cities. Professional sports. Broadway. Teachers in blue states.

When those powerhouses want something, they often can get it, and quickly. In the fall of 2022, a union drive was launched among minor league baseball players. Keeping with my brilliant capacity for prognostication, I predicted at the time that it would be a long, difficult slog that might take years. Over 5,000 professional athletes, playing in parks in almost every state in the union. It could—should—have been a nightmare of an organizing effort. But the Major League Baseball Players Association (MLBPA) put its weight behind it, and a mere *seventeen days* after the drive was launched, the owners had voluntarily recognized the new union. A contract was in place by the start of the next season.[5] My "Unionize the Minors" T-shirt was out of date before it arrived in the mail.

Hollywood is one of these powerhouses.

The biggest weakness of Hollywood's unions, though, is that pesky plural noun. The Culinary Workers are one single union, representing nearly every worker on the Strip. Hollywood has more than one. And Hollywood bosses have gotten very, very good at playing unions against each other.

In 1980, the actors struck without even telling some of the other unions. Members of the International Association of Theatrical and Stage Employees (IATSE)* formed a group to protest the strike, calling themselves WOW—We're Out of Work, openly pitting themselves against the actors.[6] That was an unforced error on the part of the unions, but it's a pattern that has repeated itself throughout Hollywood's history and one the bosses have long tried to exploit.

If you're watching unions from the sidelines, this is probably the moment you wonder why they don't just stay united. Surely, you say to yourself, they all can see this dynamic as well as I can. When unions are in conflict with each other, the boss does better. Why can't you all just get along? It's a simple solution!

To quote a favorite line of SAG president Ronald Reagan, though: Just because something is simple doesn't mean it's easy.[7]

Even when everyone's trying, unity across unions is a difficult thing to achieve. Some of it can be structural; for example, the contracts of different unions may not expire at the same time, making coordinated strikes hard to pull off. But a lot of it boils down to the reality that the different unions have different priorities at different times.

Most of this book—and most of most books about unions, to be honest—focuses on the parts of a union that are most easily observable to an outside audience. Contract fights and strikes. High-profile political battles and Supreme Court cases. New organizing and union elections.

But the actual, quotidian work of unions, the overwhelming bulk of unions' time, isn't spent on the big stuff. It's spent on little stuff—nearly invisible work that you rarely see from the outside

---

* Pronounced eye-yahtzee, basically.

and might not appreciate if you did. It's representing members facing disciplinary action. Filing grievances over the denial of someone's vacation request. Picking a new program administrator for the union-run health insurance fund. Fielding calls from members with questions about a snow day and whether they have to come in even though their kid's school is closed. Holding new member orientations. Assisting a member navigating the Americans with Disabilities Act to get an on-the-job accommodation. Double-checking membership lists in the database. Updating the website to include the name of the new shop steward. Finding a venue for the next meeting, setting up the chairs, making sure there are copies of the agenda printed. Writing up minutes of the board meeting and sending them out. Tracking down a member who's behind on dues payments. Ordering more union-branded pens. Holding mini-meetings on the shop floor to deal with an emerging problem before it turns into something that the rest of us might hear about.

The *experience* of being a union leader is much more that kind of stuff than the big, outwardly visible things.

And spending all that time on those things means unity is often nearer the bottom of your list than the top, even if it usually is on the list.

So whenever you do see unity emerge, real solidarity uniting different types of workers with different daily problems in different unions with different status levels and all the rest . . . when you see that, take note.

Be Sure to Go to the Membership Meeting Because If You're Not There You'll Get Elected President

On paper, the American labor movement is one of the most functionally democratic institutions in the country. You have hundreds of thousands of elected offices at all levels, from the treasurer of a twelve-member union of school secretaries to presidents of hundred-thousand-member locals spanning multiple states, to international officers running the whole show. Nearly all of those positions are either directly elected by the members or elected by convention delegates who in turn were elected by members. It's a cornucopia of democratic forms and functions.

Except not really.

In practice, it's really hard to get people to run for union office. Most positions are filled without a competitive election. The reasons vary. In the case of a small union, a common problem is that no one wants the job. Being the president of a small local union is something you have to do on your own time, unpaid, for which you receive minimal training and insufficient support. Your power to do things is minimal but everyone expects you to be able to solve their problems.

In the case of big union offices, it's sometimes the opposite problem. The job is so big, so powerful, so overwhelming that you can't just wake up one morning and decide to run and have any kind of chance. Incumbents have tremendous advantages that they can use to limit the chances of challengers, so there's often little incentive to try.

Now, to say that a lot of union positions don't have competitive elections is *not* the same thing as saying there's no politics. Most leaders of large locals or internationals spend much of their time building and maintaining their base of support through politicking. They appoint their rivals to key positions to placate them. They shift their strategy after they get booed at a membership meeting. And seemingly placid union conventions—when floor votes are all unanimous and it seems little is going on—are often hotbeds of backroom bargaining and conflict.

What this amounts to is that political participation happens differently in unions than in the U.S. electoral realm. In the labor movement, you don't have political parties. Even when you have strong reform movements, like we saw in chapter 6 with the Teamsters and chapter 8 with the UAW, they ebb and flow with ease, rarely seeking and almost never building a durable political infrastructure that reaches out across the whole union. A union might see a sudden fury of contests and challenges and then go years in placid contentment. Even the most long-lasting and noteworthy internal union reform movement, Teamsters for a Democratic Union, doesn't behave at all like the Democrats or Republicans do.

The biggest exception, probably the closest thing to traditional electoral politics in the labor movement, is SAG-AFTRA. There, two political parties have engaged in pitched battles for the union's leadership at all levels for years.

"Rhetoric of Hate"

When SAG-AFTRA was created in 2012 by the merger of the two unions, the internal politics of the much-larger Screen Actors Guild spilled over into the new union. Two parties, Unite for Strength and Membership First, had been around officially for at least a decade by then, though there has been factional conflict within SAG for much longer. One of the most celebrated leaders of Membership First, Ed Asner, won the election for SAG president in 1981 in a wake of backlash to the settlement of the 1980 actors' strike that we mentioned earlier.

To an outside observer, understanding the differences between a union's two political parties is a daunting task. I'm not going to try. There are differences, and for members of SAG-AFTRA they absolutely matter. The handling of health care for older actors, safety during COVID, and on-set sexual and racial harassment, pensions, residual formulas . . . there's a lot for actors to disagree on. We're just not going to spend a lot of time on it here.

Broadly speaking, Membership First is strong in the union's heartland—Hollywood and Los Angeles—while Unite for

Strength is larger in the rest of the country. For the lifetime of the merged union, Unite for Strength has won the presidency every time—Ken Howard first, then Gabrielle Carteris, then Fran Drescher—but the elections have always been close. Even more notably, while Membership First has not won the presidency of the merged SAG-AFTRA, it has several times won the union's No. 2 office, secretary-treasurer, suggesting perhaps that some share of the membership wants both sides to share power, though the two parties don't want to.

It's not just that the elections are close. They are, frankly, pretty nasty. The 2019 election, which Gabrielle Carteris won, led to charges that the conveniently timed airing of a *Beverly Hills, 90210* sequel in which Carteris played the leader of a fictional actors' union was a de facto campaign commercial for Unite for Strength.[8] The 2021 campaign witnessed escalating "rhetoric of hate" by members of both parties.[9] Old tweets by candidates with disturbing views, pictures of candidates with cult members, allegations of vote rigging . . . there was all of that and more. And for all the stuff that made it into public view, there was clearly much worse whispered on film sets and in green rooms, poisonous rhetoric that went much further than just the regular political back-and-forth. These folks meant business.

Fran Drescher of Unite for Strength—whose titular character in the 1990s sitcom *The Nanny* famously refused to cross a picket line in an episode—won the 2021 election, defeating her opponent from Membership First, Matthew Modine, but the secretary-treasurer position was won by Membership First's Joely Fisher. The campaign, it seems, never really ended after that. The sniping and politicking continued.

It was the middle of COVID pandemic, and both sides accused the other of disregarding members' safety. Hollywood was also in the midst of a whole series of #MeToo scandals involving prominent actors, directors, and producers, and the responses of the union became political fodder. As the two sides sniped, we settled in for another binge-watch of *Game of Thrones,* and the bosses counted their growing profits.

Aside from the day-to-day challenges in building union solidarity, it's hard to let go of a grudge. Union leaders are every bit as human as the rest of us. SAG-AFTRA's party leaders had said a lot of things that couldn't be unsaid.

But It Was Also 2023

At other times. the poisonous relationship between Membership First and Unite for Strength may have been enough to doom unity efforts. In 2023? Not so much.

The same things that we've seen throughout this book were present in Hollywood, too. As billionaires only got richer as regular Americans dealt with the pandemic, the recession, the inflation, and the threat of incipient fascism, the workers in the entertainment industry got as angry as everyone else did. And, like grad employees or Frito-Lay workers, they turned in the direction of solidarity.

As the agreements between the studios and the writers and actors came up for renewal in 2023, things began shifting. Everywhere you looked, workers were finding their way toward each other. Unions were showing more and more solidarity. Take the Teamsters, whose members in its Motion Picture Division drive trucks, handle props, and even train animals. A strike by writers or actors would impact their jobs, and, in previous Hollywood strikes, such behind-the-scenes unions were often left behind. But Motion Picture Division director Lindsay Dougherty was vocal in her support for the writers and actors. "What I'd like to say to the studios," she told a Writers Guild* meeting, "is: 'If you want

---

* There are, confusingly, two Writers Guilds—Writers Guild of America, West, and Writers Guild of America, East. They are autonomous organizations with their

to fuck around, you're gonna find out.'"[10] IATSE and the other unions, stung in the past by actors and writers going off on their own, pledged their support.

But all of that pales in comparison to what happened within SAG-AFTRA.

Here's the thing about internal union political maneuvers: Unless you were in the room where it happened, you don't know how it went down. Unions organize in secret. They always have.[11] And, on something so politically sensitive as this, that secrecy is taken even more seriously.

We know some of it. It seems like SAG-AFTRA president Fran Drescher and secretary Joely Fisher were the driving forces, and we know the titular head of Membership First, Matthew Modine, wasn't on board, because he split from his own party over the issue and didn't back it. But we don't know much else—its terms, what it portended for the future, whether it marked a permanent cessation of hostilities or a temporary alliance.

The "it" was a unity ticket. Membership First suggested postponing the elections, but that didn't fly, and when it didn't, unity was the answer.[12] For the 2023 elections, Unite for Strength and Membership First put aside their rivalry and agreed on a joint leadership slate. Drescher and Fisher would stay in their existing roles, and the two parties divided up seats on the union's executive board. They would go into the 2023 strike without the distraction of a competitive, potentially nasty, election dividing them.*

---

own internal structures, with a dividing line at the Mississippi River. However, they have formal affiliation agreements with each other and a long history of close cooperation, meaning that, while it is inaccurate to refer to the Writers Guild in the singular, it's a shorthand that we can use without doing too much damage to the truth.

* It has to be said, this decision prompts interesting questions about the nature of union democracy. After all, the leaders of Membership First and Unite for Strength effectively cut rank-and-file members out of the process and imposed a leadership ticket from above. Is that what a democratic labor movement should want? Some

And so, SAG-AFTRA didn't have a hotly contested, vitriolic race.* Instead, the leaders went into the strike able to focus on the conflict with the bosses.

And what a strike. SAG-AFTRA has 160,000 members, the Writers Guild another 30,000 or so, making it the largest strike since the UPS strike in 1997 (or, just before season five of *The Nanny* premiered, if that's how you keep track of time). As with the other big strikes of 2023, the public swung behind the workers right from the beginning.

This was, in no small part, because the studio execs were unable to persuade anyone of their supposed poverty. This has been a recurring feature of this labor resurgence, and a marked shift from strikes earlier in the 2000s. Corporate America has lost—for how long, I dare not guess—the ability to scare the public into believing that treating workers fairly will put them out of business.

The actors and the writers came away from the strike with solid wins.[13] Higher pay, better control over their work, and measures to make sets safer are all good things. The unions both ratified their contracts by large margins, which generally means the members are satisfied.

It's also true, though, that the challenges haven't disappeared. In addition to streaming, and the ever-shifting tastes of the public, entertainment unions are now confronted with the risk that artificial intelligence (AI) will render them redundant. The election

---

key leaders weren't having it. Matthew Modine (through his publicist—this *is* Hollywood, after all) declared that "Membership First no longer exists" though it's not clear it was his decision to make.[3] Even though they were denied the Membership First–Unite for Strength showdown they'd been expecting, it seems like the members were happy with the deal.

* Drescher and Fisher did each draw an opponent, running as independents, but the race was never close and the campaign was much quieter than in the past. Matthew Modine ended up running on his own for a seat on the Los Angeles local board, coming in twenty-fifth, which was still enough to win a seat on the forty-five-member board, but it must have been a bit of a letdown.

of Donald Trump has meant that regulatory efforts to rein in AI have stalled or stopped altogether, and corporations are pushing the envelope every day, using AI to write scripts, draw animation, provide special effects, and reincarnate long-dead celebrities. Film and TV producers continue to find new ways to make money by sticking it to the workers, and the unions will have to respond. They have no call to rest easy just because of one successful (huge, popular, inspiring) strike. Any contract between unions and bosses is just a truce.

That's a lesson that the labor movement often forgets. Perhaps the greatest mistake of the leaders of labor's Golden Age—symbolized in 1950's Treaty of Detroit, as we discussed in chapter 2—is that too many came to believe that the fundamental conflict between workers and bosses was settled permanently. It's easy to see why; through the 1950s and 1960s, unions stayed strong, politicians of all stripes supported them, and the big industrial powerhouses driving the American economy, especially in steel and automobiles, seemed to have found a modus vivendi with unions. Even incredibly disruptive events, like the 1959 steel strike that lasted 116 days, didn't appear to disrupt the postwar labor-management consensus.

In reality, corporate America never consented to that consensus. For a while, when it seemed like companies didn't have the power to fight back, they hunkered down and played nice, and thereby lulled too many in organized labor to sleep. By the time labor woke up to see the ground shifting under their feet, it was too late to stop the antiunion wave of the 1980s and 1990s.

But the unions of Hollywood, more than the rest of the labor movement, never got that comfortable. Their industry was too visibly and too rapidly changing. They never had a long period of calm. The film and television industry is constantly in a state of reinvention, and that reinvention has real-life impacts on all who work in it. The unions have always known they needed to be able to organize to face newer, different threats. Eternal vigilance is the price of their union strength.

That's why, surely, the biggest win from the 2023 writers and actors' strikes was the solidarity. Unity across the industry and unity within its largest union is the best way for actors, writers, gaffers, painters, set dressers, costumers, camera operators, best boys, and all the other job titles we see in the closing credits to get their fair share. SAG-AFTRA will, I'm sure, continue to have knock-down, drag-out leadership elections in the years to come. That's perhaps as it should be—there are clearly issues to debate and discuss. But, for a little while at least, the studio executives might see that those disagreements can and will be set aside when the members need to band together. Solidarity conquers all.

8

It Doesn't Have to Be This Way

The United Auto Workers union was the main character in America's labor movement for at least twenty-five years. Few expected it to reclaim the role in 2023.

The founders of the CIO, had they had their pick, probably would have chosen steel rather than auto as their poster child. The Flint Sit-Down Strike changed that. The change was cemented by the postwar suburban housing boom and the construction of the interstate highway system. The car became indispensable, and the auto industry and its union the engine of the American economy.

The Treaty of Detroit was just the most visible symbol of the UAW's dominance, but we've seen its echoes throughout this book, from the UAW's financial support of the AFT to its sponsorship of the 1963 March on Washington to the union's key role in higher education organizing. Our entire understanding of unions—what they do, how they look, who's in them, what they mean—is still based in no small part on the glory days of the UAW in the 1950s and 1960s.

That was a long time ago.

The UAW's dynamic, larger-than-life leader, Walter Reuther, died in a plane crash in 1970.* Two years later, the Lordstown

---

* I try to avoid conspiracy theories, but the specific cause of the plane crash Reuther died in—altimeter malfunction—had been the cause of another crash involving Reuther not that long before, one that he'd survived, and in both cases the crash came after the plane left the same airport, and, well, you do have to wonder.

(Ohio) strike highlighted the degree to which manufacturing jobs were becoming increasingly intolerable, dangerous, and monotonous, no longer worth the trade-offs of the Treaty of Detroit.[1] In the 1980s and 1990s, foreign competition, corporate greed, and antiworker trade policies led to a collapse in the domestic auto industry. The UAW had one-and-a-half-million members in 1979, almost all working for the Big Three automakers (at the time, GM, Ford, and Chrysler; Chrysler's gone through many ownership changes and these days lives on as Stellantis). By 2023, its membership was barely one-quarter of that. The union was reeling from the years-long corruption scandal involving Fiat Chrysler, a scandal that had sent many of its top officials to prison. Nonunionized auto companies like Elon Musk's Tesla were on the rise. The UAW was, you might understandably have thought, slowly fading away into irrelevance.

And then the UAW went ahead and launched the most ambitious and successful strike of the twenty-first century.

Nothing better encapsulates the resurgence of organized labor than the revitalization of the United Auto Workers and their 2023 strike. It was the culmination of everything we've talked about—the challenges and corporate disrespect of the COVID era, the jolt of energy brought into the movement by younger workers, the reinvention of the old establishment of labor.

Sitting here, now, it can feel like that strike was almost inevitable, the natural outcome of the political, economic, and social context in which the UAW operated. Nonsense. There very easily could have been a world where the UAW didn't strike, or struck and got crushed, and it would have looked more or less the same as this one up to that point. The UAW's 2023 contract campaign against the Big Three automakers wasn't just the result of time and place. It was a brilliantly conceived effort, flawlessly executed by tens of thousands of union members. It had the panache of the Dartmouth graduate workers, the passionate intensity of striking teachers, the political savvy of the flight attendants, and the determination of Frito-Lay workers. It really was that big of a deal.

So, how did it happen?

Reforming the UAW

As I began doing more writing, even occasionally getting paid for it, I wanted to make sure I was supporting other writers, so, on October 21, 2014, I joined the National Writers Union (NWU). I didn't really remark upon it at the time, but the NWU was also known as Local 1981 of the United Auto Workers.

When disparate groups of UAW members around the country began coalescing in 2018 and 2019, one of the people involved was Labor Notes staffer Chris Brooks, who'd written damning indictments of the UAW's unsuccessful campaigns to organize the Volkswagen plant in Chattanooga, Tennessee, in 2014 and 2019. Because I'd written a few things for Labor Notes, Chris invited me to one of the very first meetings of what became Unite All Workers for Democracy (UAWD).

This would be the perfect moment for me to share some there-at-the-beginning memories of the UAWD. I could talk about the first time I heard someone named Shawn Fain on one of the conference calls, or maybe when the group first kicked around the idea of striking all three American automakers at the same time. That kind of thing.

But I don't know if any of that happened. I remember almost nothing of my membership in the UAWD.* I don't remember any of the conversations, who was there, what we did. It's such a letdown. What I do remember is that, with the same keen insight and understanding I've shown again and again in my time in labor, I

---

* The National Writers Union left the UAW in early 2020, and I stopped attending UAWD meetings as a result.

was pretty sure the UAWD wasn't going to go anywhere, that they were well-intentioned folks who weren't going to be able to get anything done.

For decades, the UAW had been a one-party state. The Administration Caucus, first formed by Walter Reuther himself, had been running the union for decades. There had been no serious challenge to their power through that time. Their strongest opposition was in Canada, which is a big part of the reason why the Canadian Auto Workers split off and formed their own union in the 1980s. With them gone, the Administration Caucus reigned supreme.

But the times they were a-changing. Like so many others in this book, UAW members were, regardless of their age, children of 2008. In the Great Recession, GM and Chrysler both filed for bankruptcy, and autoworkers were forced to swallow huge cuts to pay and benefits as well as the introduction of a two-tiered system that made things even worse for new hires. It was because of the financial pressures of those years, too, that Chrysler, "looking to reduce its labor costs . . . made a happy marriage" with the UAW's leaders.[2] Chrysler lavished gifts and cash on UAW leaders, and in return those leaders negotiated weak deals with the employer. Then they got caught.

The Fiat Chrysler scandal was a big deal, and not just because of the crimes. The Administration Caucus responded to the scandal by closing ranks. They said very little to the members and defended leaders who were connected to the scandal. Members who'd never paid attention to internal UAW politics saw a leadership that seemed more interested in protecting its own than in making sure the union was being run honestly.

It's not hard to imagine an alternative timeline in which the Administration Caucus makes a big show of cleaning house, takes concrete steps to engage and involve members in the work of the union, and demonstrates a deep commitment to reform. In that timeline, the UAWD maybe remains a minor nuisance to the leaders. There's perhaps a lesson there.

Major corruption in the union gave the feds justification for appointing an overseer of the union, and one of the things that the overseer suggested, and that the UAW agreed to do, was to hold a referendum on whether or not the leaders of the union should be directly elected by the membership. The UAW's top officers, like many other unions, had always been elected by delegates to the UAW's international convention, but now the members would get to vote on whether or not they would get to vote for their leaders. This will come as a great shock to you, but when union members who've never before had a direct say in who leads the union are given the opportunity to decide if *they get to decide,* they're going to take it. Something like 64 percent voted yes in the fall of 2021.

For reasons passing strange, the Administration Caucus didn't see this coming and so found itself defending a system that two-thirds of their members opposed. For the UAWD, this was manna from heaven. A referendum on direct elections is a great way for an insurgent group to organize and build support. It allows them to test the strength of their organization, to get their name out to more people, to see where the ground lay. Being on the winning side of the referendum, moreover, gave them a kind of legitimacy in the eyes of UAW members. The referendum—demanded by federal monitors, agreed to by the Administration Caucus—became the UAWD's referendum.

The Administration Caucus couldn't have bungled this more, and that very bungling was proof of how out of touch they were with their members. It's almost unavoidable that distance will open up between union members and leaders. Leaders are successful if they remain nimble, shifting their priorities and their personalities and their rhetoric based on how members react.

I remember once negotiating for a group of school employees in central Illinois. Our bargaining team was very angry with the rudeness and jackassery of the superintendent. We took the district's final offer to the members, recommending that they tell the district to go to hell and strike. The members ratified it almost unanimously. They didn't care that the superintendent was an ass. The contract offer had big raises in it and real improvements in health care, and they were happy with it. We on the negotiating team had become too insular to see that our members were not in the same place as us. This is what happened to the Administration Caucus.

Incumbency still has its advantages, though, and the UAW's elections in 2023 were incredibly close. The UAWD's endorsed candidates prevailed in the bulk of the races, and Shawn Fain was elected UAW president with 50.2 percent of the vote, not even 500 ahead of his opponent. When you break down the results, it's clear that Fain's narrow win came because he was supported not just by autoworkers—the union's core constituency—but also by the other workers that the UAW had been organizing in recent years, most notably the graduate workers. The UAW locals representing grads in Massachusetts and California went heavily for Fain and the UAWD.

The reformers had won—just. They had no time to catch their breath. Fain and his team took office just as negotiations were set to begin with the Big Three automakers. Because many UAW staff are political hires, serving at the pleasure of the leaders, there was a significant staff turnover right away, meaning the people with the most experience in negotiations were gone. The election campaign had been intense, and there wasn't even time for a lot of fence mending between the two sides. Turnout in the election, for all its importance, had been fairly low. It was by no means clear that Shawn Fain and the UAWD had the confidence of the majority of the membership.

No one would have blamed Fain and the UAWD if they had focused on getting their house in order, moving gingerly so as not to overextend themselves. That is not what they did.

What we have seen through these years of resurgence, something we had gotten used to not seeing in the labor movement, is boldness and imagination. It took moxie for Sara Nelson to stare down the aviation executives and win a better legislative package than in any other industries. It took vision and ambition for Starbucks Workers United to see one little win in Buffalo and dive headfirst into a sprawling national campaign. It took genuine courage for Frito-Lay workers, who had relatively decent jobs for their community, put it all on the line to strike for better working conditions. It took fierce bravery for Amulya Mandava, Margaret Czerwienski, Sasha Brietzke, and others to challenge the sexual harassment culture of their campuses. All of these folks, and so many more, found in the solidarity of the movement the power to act. And they acted magnificently.

Now the UAW would get its chance to be bold, in its contract campaigns against the Big Three.

A Brief History of Contract Campaigns

So, we need to talk about contract campaigns a bit. We've alluded to them here and there in the book, but we need to dive a little deeper, because it really matters. This may feel too inside-baseball for many of you, and maybe it is, but the UAW contract campaign wasn't something involving a few dozen key leaders and staff. It extended and expanded to eventually involve hundreds of thousands of people, most of them not even UAW members. So remember as you read about this: If you're the kind of person who would read this book, there's a pretty good chance you were a part of the UAW contract campaign, whether you knew it or not.

A lot of people who are unfamiliar with union negotiations tend to think the action happens at the negotiating table. Witty verbal repartee, well-chosen bon mots, cunning arguments, that kind of thing. You can get a better contract, the thinking goes, if you win the battle of wits. Show the other side how wrong they are, maybe even humiliate them with some kind of *West Wing* monologue, and they'll have no choice but to accede to your demands.

No.

Really, no.

Here's how the at-the-table part of negotiations works:

1. You hand them a piece of paper with a proposal on it.
2. They leave the room and talk about your proposal.
3. They come back in the room and hand you a different piece of paper, responding to your proposal or maybe bringing up something new.
4. You leave the room to talk about their piece of paper.
5. Lather, rinse, repeat.

The bulk of your time in negotiations is spent waiting around for them to get back to you or for you to get back to them. Sure, sometimes you can have substantive conversations at the bargaining table, and, yes, every once in a while those conversations—on their own—move the needle in negotiations, but not often. The people on the other side of the table rarely have the authority to agree to much without leaving the room and talking to other people, so even if you do get into a big verbal jousting match and rhetorically knock them off their high horses, it won't result in them caving; they'll go into the other room and come back and act like it never happened.

It still matters what happens at the bargaining table. You still need skilled and able negotiators to make your case crisply and clearly. You need folks good at writing and comprehending contract language, so you don't agree to something that doesn't mean what you think it means. You need to be able to pick up on shifts in the other side's language, to notice the hints they may drop or the openness they may show. You need to be able to maintain a certain amount of civility even in the face of implacable hostility, so that when things get to the end you can work through the final details with them.

So when I say to people that you could have trained squirrels at the bargaining table for your union and you'd get the same result as if you had the smoothest negotiators in the world, I am exaggerating quite a bit. But it's absolutely true that contracts aren't won or lost at the bargaining table.

What happens away from the table matters so much more, and that's the contract campaign. The contract campaign is where you exercise power.

What kind of power, applied in what manner, is sufficient to get the other side to give you what you want? The correct answer, at least before you start planning, is that you have no idea. You don't know what it's going to take to get things done. You don't know which leverage point will work and which won't. You also don't know how far the other side will be willing or able to move even if you have the power to make them.

This all means a key phase of any contract campaign is research. You've got to look at every possible angle: Every financial relationship the company has. Every product it produces or service it provides. The details of every senior executive, every board member. The nuances of every law surrounding the kind of work being done at this workplace. The particularities of the localities where the work is done. Who supplies the company, and who in turn the company supplies. Which political leaders the bosses are close to, and who they have beef with. And so much more.

The thinking is this: You've got to figure all this stuff out because, in your contract campaign, you've got to try it all.[3] Can't stress this enough: *You don't know what will work.*

Back in the salad days of the 1950s, the general presumption was that the tool the unions had was the strike. The union walks out, and then it's a battle of attrition—the company's capacity to absorb losses as the strike wears on versus the workers' capacity to stay on the picket line. You had professors of industrial relations who wrote books on this sort of thing, treating it almost as a mathematical formula: *worker strike fund minus corporate losses equals whoever will win.*

But the strike was never the perfect weapon. This became especially true after Reagan fired the air traffic controllers in 1981. As we've noted, that event was the starter pistol for an aggressive corporate offensive against unions.

A key element in that offensive was the permanent worker replacement. You see, it's illegal for a company to fire workers for striking; it's legally protected activity.* But while the courts have long affirmed that right, the Supreme Court also said, way back in the 1930s, that a company could replace a striking worker, and do so permanently. How is that not firing, you may ask? A worker who is permanently replaced still has the right, after the strike is over, to get a job back at the company, but only when there are vacancies. Striking workers have no legal right to kick out the replacement workers to take back their jobs. That's the distinction.

Now, this option had been sitting around since the 1930s, but companies had only rarely used it. It's not clear why; perhaps they were worried that aggressively replacing striking workers would lead Congress to ban the practice. By the 1980s, though, permanent replacements were regularly employed by companies, and the strike, as a weapon, declined in strategic importance.

Lots of other contract campaign strategies began to be employed. So-called "corporate campaigns" targeted a company's board of directors with public actions designed to hurt the company's reputation or lose potential business. Unions became more savvy about

---

* This is very much *not* true for the public sector, where workers (like the air traffic controllers) can indeed be fired for striking, depending on the specific state or federal public employee labor law in a given situation.

enlisting local notables, like church leaders or mayors, to support the workers during a campaign. They played to politicians. They became experts on environmental and financial regulation and would sic the government on a company until the company made a deal. And on and on.

These contract campaign strategies have often been inventive, imaginative, creative, and even fun. When a school board member told a unit of school bus drivers, during negotiations, that a monkey could do their job, we ordered five hundred stuffed monkeys from a carnival supply store, and the drivers handed them to kids with a note for their parents as they got off the bus. The contract was settled quickly.

But let's say it again: You don't know what's going to work.

Companies are very good at countering these moves. They launch their own attacks, too; when a union pushes hard on things like environmental laws, it's not uncommon for employers to call it extortion, and sometimes even take the union to court over it. They spend their own money to buy community support. They delay, obfuscate, bluster . . . eight chapters into this book, you know the drill.

And so the best contract campaigns don't rely upon one or two key strategies. They use them all. They plan to work every possible angle, to be doing, as the movie title puts it, everything, everywhere, all at once.

No one who works on labor issues disagrees that contract campaigns need to be sophisticated, well-planned, and carefully executed. And yet, we don't do that a lot. Why?

There are plenty of reasons—time and resources are of course critical—but one of the biggest ones, and the one most relevant to the UAW's contract campaign, is a lack of trust in members.

The thing about most of these strategic campaign ideas is that it's very, very easy to plan them in a little war room with a few key leaders and staff. And sometimes, while you're building those castles in the air, you get high on your own supply, and begin to believe that your plan is so damned smart that regular old members can't be trusted to carry it out. They're not savvy enough, you might think. Or, if you're a little more self-aware than that, your fallback is that, sure, workers are intelligent, but they haven't been part of all these planning sessions. It's just too much work to explain it to them all. They'd never have the time and perspective to understand it all, and even if they did, the risk is too high that the bosses will find out.* And even if they understood it, it's too difficult for them to carry out. The plans are too elaborate, too bold—they're better off just waiting for specific directives from us. It's too bad, because we all believe in our members. Just, this time, they're going to have to trust us to do this for them.

For union leaders used to decades of retreat, another seeming risk of inviting the members into the process was that you might raise their expectations higher than was reasonable. Members who have an inflated sense of what's possible are wont to jump into precipitate actions, like the air traffic controllers in 1981. Better to dampen their hopes from the get-go, so that they don't get too upset when they don't get much.†

---

* For those playing at home: When a union leader or staffer tells you they're keeping something from the members so that the boss won't find out, that's the way you know they're full of it. Spoiler alert: The boss already knows. The massive union-busting industry has written whole playbooks on how to fight unions (remember "violate the law here"?) and have gamed out all the scenarios. Often the people most in the dark are the members themselves. The only exceptions I'll allow are for very time-sensitive matters—it might be best if the boss doesn't know the exact time of your instant strike—or for acts of civil disobedience and the details of legal filings.

† It's easy to sneer at this attitude, and sneering really is the right thing to do, but there's also this: In many industries, for many decades, leaders were right to keep member expectations low. Public support for unions was generally low in the 1980s, 1990s, and 2000s. Politicians weren't willing to stick their necks out for unions. Corporations union-busted like crazy and got away with it. Survival *was* victory in some of those cases. Taking a big gamble in the hopes of something bigger might have destroyed your union, as with the Hormel workers in Austin, Minnesota. I've never met a union leader or staffer who *enjoyed* snuffing out members' hopes, but I've known many who thought it was necessary, and at some times in the not-too-distant past, it may have been.

Therefore, contract campaigns are too often hampered by an unwillingness to trust the members to do their part. And that means you're leaving most of your options on the cutting room floor.

Shawn Fain had just won a tight race to be UAW president. A fair number of UAW locals representing big auto plants voted against him, and the side that lost wasn't showing any interest in going down quietly. It would have been political suicide for Fain to make his contract campaign strategy contingent on trusting those same locals, right? Right?

Except that we were in the most prolabor moment of our lifetimes. As we've seen throughout this book, labor wins that would have been unthinkable a decade earlier became almost routine in the first half of the 2020s. It was the time to take the chance on asking your strongest supporters not to vote, to form a unity ticket with your mortal enemies inside the union, and to walk out for things that will only benefit your students.

It was the time to trust the members who voted against you to have your back when you take the fight to the bosses.

The Campaign

From the very beginning, by refusing to shake the hands of the auto company executives, Shawn Fain set a different tone in 2023's auto negotiations. Of course, he wasn't taking bribes from those executives, so he probably didn't feel as much pressure to shake their hands.

You can argue that such a gesture was just that, a gesture, without any real meaning. Refusing to shake hands doesn't demonstrate any real power, after all. It's just theatricality. No boss is going to give up more in contract negotiations in hope of a handshake.

Fain and his team knew better than that. The goal wasn't to intimidate the bosses. It was to send a message to the members.

The UAW ran its contract campaign—purposefully, I suspect—in such a way as to prioritize connection with its members, because it knew it would need all members to be on board as things got tougher. "We need to run contract campaigns where we engage the membership and go after their demands," Fain told a reporter.[4]

The UAW wasn't just negotiating over wages, health care, and pensions. They weren't just trying to undo two-tier systems that had been agreed to after the Great Recession. They were also focused on the future—electric vehicles. By mid-2023, when these negotiations were in full swing, Biden's Inflation Reduction Act had passed, and it contained all kinds of goodies for the electric-vehicle industry. It was vital for the UAW's survival in the auto industry to make sure that, when the Big Three built electric vehicles, they would be built in UAW-represented facilities.

They also needed to stop the bleeding caused by ongoing plant closures.

I grew up in the northwest suburbs of Chicago. Whenever we got in the car to head to Wisconsin, or when I drove to college in Minnesota, I'd take I-90, and drive right by the massive Chrysler plant in Belvidere, Illinois. It's right along the highway, and every time I'd drive by, it was a beehive of activity, just endless acres of cars waiting to get shipped around the country.

Stellantis, the successor to Chrysler, had closed the plant, scattering its workers all over. Many of those Belvidere workers had come there from other closed plants in Ohio and elsewhere. The UAW contract gave those workers rights to move to jobs at other plants, but that's cold comfort when you've left your family and life behind and are living out of a studio apartment in a strange city. The UAW wanted to protect the right to strike during the life of the contract in order to prevent plant closures, and they wanted some of the closed plants reopened.

Fain had hired Labor Notes staffer Jonah Furman to run the union's communications department; the UAW rolled out well-produced videos highlighting members' work and their demands.

Unions had long been behind the curve in video, never giving it enough attention. More Perfect Union, a prounion organization founded by former Bernie Sanders staffers after the 2020 election, raised the bar, producing powerful, high-quality videos of the miners' strike at Warrior Met and the 2021 Amazon election in Bessemer, Alabama, among others. The UAW's videos were perfect for sharing on social media, short and snappy. It's not like making videos was some kind of secret hitherto unknown to labor, but More Perfect Union and the UAW showed why it mattered.

The UAW took an aggressive, populist tack in its messages. Gone were union nostrums about healthy cooperation with the auto companies and the mutual interests between labor and management. Instead, the UAW railed against the billions in profits the auto companies were making, excoriated the lavish lifestyles of the rich, and openly called for the workers to get their fair share of the pie. Once again, like refusing the handshake, this could easily look like posturing to outside eyes. The members, though, had been telling each other the same things around the metaphorical water cooler for years. These messages fired them up and raised their expectations. They also set the table for the next phase; by the time the automakers began aggressively making their own case to the public, the union had already set the narrative.

The Strike

While Fain and his team were negotiating hard, other leaders and staff were preparing for the next phase.

Afterward, it was not uncommon to see media reports suggest that the UAW had never really been trying to reach a deal at the bargaining table, that it had only been buying time while it prepared for a strike that it was going to launch no matter what.[5] That's a basic misunderstanding of what the UAW was doing, but it's not a surprising take.

In the case of most negotiations, unions don't begin planning for a strike until negotiations are far advanced and there's decreasing hope of a settlement. This is largely a walk-and-chew-gum thing; negotiations are generally seen as something that takes all a union's time, so there's no energy left for also planning a strike. It also has a psychological component. Very few people are built temperamentally to *want* to go on strike. We've seen this throughout the book—workers are very anxious about striking (understandably so) and will often go to great lengths to avoid having to do it, so planning for it can make them anxious and cause them to take their eye off the ball. Moreover, once a union strikes, it has basically played all its cards. For the union, the strike is the ultimate escalation, and one that you can't really back down from.

For all these reasons and more, even big and powerful strikes are usually planned pretty late in the day. The UAW didn't do that. It planned for a possible strike alongside the negotiations. Rather than read this as a sign of bad faith on the union's part, recognize it for what it really was: a union that had its act together.

The strike that finally launched on September 15, 2023, was unlike any other UAW strike in two monumentally important ways. First, it struck all three auto companies at once. Second, it didn't strike everywhere. Both decisions were brilliant gambles.

The general UAW practice over the decades had been to whipsaw the three companies against each other during negotiations. Use a win at one table and push it on the other companies, and if one of the companies was falling behind the others, that's the one you struck, to get it in line. An automaker had a stronger incentive to settle the strike when its plants weren't producing anything and its competitors were happily at work, pumping out new cars and taking away business. Also, while the UAW's $825 million strike fund was easily the largest in organized labor, it would evaporate pretty quickly if there was a sustained strike involving more than one automaker.

As you can see, the idea of striking only one company had some pretty solid logic behind it. It was hardly a terrible idea. But it had its downsides. It made the messaging harder. If all three auto companies are greedy and not giving workers what they deserve, why strike only one? It also allowed the media and others to portray the strike as limited and focused, a conflict between just one company and the union rather than a struggle for the whole working class. And, by 2024, it was silly to pretend that the only players in auto were GM, Ford, and Stellantis. Toyota, Honda, BMW, Hyundai, and all the rest were going to keep making cars no matter who was on strike.

Striking all three companies at once offered some real opportunities. The whipsawing tried during negotiations could continue during a strike, as each company had an incentive to settle first. It also made for a very straightforward David vs. Goliath story, the kind of story the UAW had been pushing strongly from the beginning. And it raised the stakes of the strike; it made people and groups who otherwise might have had an excuse to look the other way take a side. The historic nature of the strike meant lots of people, like prominent prolabor politicians, had to sit up and take notice.

But the strike fund was still a real concern. With something around 150,000 members at all three automakers, the union's $500 a week in strike pay would add up to $75 million or so a week if everyone went out. And it was still true that if everyone went out on strike, there were few escalatory options left.

The solution was brilliant, the kind of brilliant that, once you hear about it, seems so obvious as to appear commonplace. The Association of Flight Attendants, as we saw in chapter 3, had taken advantage of the Railway Labor Act to launch intermittent strikes through its CHAOS plan. The UAW didn't have the legal right to launch intermittent strikes but still wanted a way to create its own kind of lower-case chaos. The answer was the Stand-Up Strike.

At 10 p.m. on the night of September 14, Shawn Fain appeared on Facebook Live and announced the plan. The union was striking all three automakers, but only one plant each, in Michigan, Missouri, and Ohio.[6] The 13,000 workers themselves only got a few hours' notice that they were going to be striking.

At the same time the first UAW members walked out, the union launched an intensive member education effort to explain the strike strategy and the legal rights of all union members under expired union contracts. This legal strategy was one purpose-built to appeal to hard core labor nerds like me, inspired by the brilliant strategies in lawyer David Rosenfeld's pamphlet/book, *Offensive Bargaining.** The strategy depended on members being vigilant on the job, keeping in touch with the union, and gave all members a chance to be involved even if their plant wasn't on strike.

The public-facing aspect of the campaign was equally impressive. Shawn Fain's Facebook videos quickly became viral favorites of labor supporters; all of us helped spread those messages. The huge profits earned by the auto companies meant that their pleas of poverty were largely ignored. Because only three plants were on strike at first, it meant that nationwide strike story still had a sort of local dimension to it. The media congregated around these sites, where autoworkers obligingly supplied endless quotes echoing the union's messages. The peak of the public strategy, of course, was when Joe Biden became the first president in U.S. history to walk a striking union's picket line.[†]

---

* For years, you could only buy a copy of *Offensive Bargaining* if you could establish to the publisher that you were on the side of organized labor. Even if you were a union member, you had to demonstrate your commitment to the movement; some people I knew needed references from other union folks to be allowed to buy the book. They didn't want copies to fall into the hands of management. Then someone put it up as a PDF some years ago, and now you can get it with a quick internet search. Takes away some of the spy-novel romance of the book, but it's still worth a read.

† The shift in Democratic Party attitudes toward unions has been welcome but

Crucial to this was the deep trust the UAW put in all its members. Walking out of your plant while knowing most of the other plants were still open is its own kind of scary. But the intense political education the union had been doing was paying off. The reason strikers on the picket line gave such good quotes to the press wasn't because they were planted by the union, but because the union had done such a good job building a message that matched members' own beliefs. They couldn't help but be on-message.

The importance of trusting the members was highlighted again when the next round of plant strikes was called. Again, workers were given only a few hours' notice, and yet, once again, they all walked off the job together. It's easy to imagine a world where this goes wrong, where workers, not given a lot of notice, refuse to strike and go in to work. Instead, they all walked out.

I met some of them on a picket line at a Stellantis parts facility. They were almost all men, almost all in their fifties, and none of them had ever been on strike before. Several of them had been at that facility for only a few months, having transferred there when their regular jobs in Belvidere, Illinois, were cut. They'd had no idea they were going to get the call. By and large, they liked their managers; everyone got along there. And, apparently, for a few minutes after the call came in, those managers tried to talk the UAW members out of striking. Didn't work.

The bind this strategy created for the automakers was a joy to behold. Because these companies run such tightly integrated systems, striking just one plant had almost as much of an impact on the company's bottom line as striking them all, and yet the companies still had to continue paying the majority of their workers in the other plants. The unemployment rate was low, and

surprising. Bill and Hillary Clinton, infamously, crossed a union picket line on their very first date (see Zach Schwartz-Weinstein, "On Bill and Hillary Clinton's First Date in 1971, They Crossed a Picket Line," *In These Times* (February 9, 2016), inthesetimes.com/article/hillary-rodham-bill-clinton-and-the-1971-yale-strike).

a higher share of people between the ages of twenty-five and fifty-four were working than at any point in the entire twenty-first century, so if the company had tried to find replacement workers they would have had their hands full. They could have called the UAW's bluff and locked out the remaining workers, but under the NLRA, a locked-out worker cannot be permanently replaced, meaning the companies couldn't play their strongest union-busting card.

The companies were wholly unprepared for the Stand-Up Strike. As the weeks went by, the UAW played the companies against each other: When one company gave a little more at the bargaining table, it wouldn't have a facility included in the next round of walkouts. The UAW began changing the rhythm, too, calling out plants at unexpected times. On Wednesday, October 11, sitting across the bargaining table from Ford's executives, Shawn Fain received the company's latest economic offer, showing no change, and he and his team immediately walked out of the negotiations. As he rose, he told the Ford negotiators, "This just cost you Kentucky Truck Plant," and within *ten minutes* the workers were streaming out of one of Ford's signature facilities.[7]

When I was union leader at the University of Illinois in the late 1990s, we used to dream about what we called a Pied Piper strike: Just start walking down the halls, calling to the instructors, "We're going on strike right now," and have them all follow us onto the picket line. It was a dream because there was no way that could happen. There was zero chance that with just a few minutes' warning, workers—even workers strongly committed to the union—would be willing to upend their lives by walking off the job. Could. Not. Happen. Unless, apparently, you were a UAW member at the Kentucky Truck Plant.

As the days went by, the concessions trickled in, as the companies threw more and more things on the table in an attempt to end the strike. The UAW likely could have stopped the strike earlier and still called it a win, but it held out long enough to win a contract so powerful as to beggar the imagination.

End of two-tier wage scales, and a boost in the starting wage to over $30 an hour. The return of annual cost-of-living adjustments (the signature achievement of the Treaty of Detroit). The right to strike over plant closures. Increased pension contributions. Agreements by the companies to put their EV plants under the master contract, or at least to make it easier for the union to organize them.

And the reopening of the Belvidere Stellantis plant.

That's never happened before.

It doesn't have to be this way. Workers can fight and workers can win.

In a movement this big, this diverse, there are always glimmers of hope, always moments that maybe, just maybe, herald something bigger. The 1997 Teamsters strike at UPS was one of those moments. So was the Occupy movement in 2011 and the Red for Ed teacher strikes in 2018. But, for all the excitement they generated and all the real gains they helped make, they didn't change the trajectory. We'd hoped they'd build and keep going, and by and large they didn't.

All those false dawns, though, leave their traces behind them. You can find Occupy veterans in unions across the country, and in groups like the Emergency Workplace Organizing Committee (EWOC), which helps workers without a union stand up and fight. The lessons learned from the 1997 Teamsters strike directly influenced the 2023 UPS negotiations. Some number of Red for Ed teachers have second jobs at Starbucks, and have done their part. And so on. Everything echoes, bouncing along across time and place.

The last few years, though, have been nothing like those moments. A sustained, ongoing, thriving labor movement has been gaining in power and (perhaps more important) confidence. New leaders have been stepping to the fore, and they are more ambitious, more energizing, and more visionary than what went before. Their vision comes, in part, from the events they themselves have been a part of. It's easier to be a visionary when you've seen change happening before your eyes.

Workers—I hesitate to ever use a term like "ordinary workers," but you know what I mean—have found themselves taking on their bosses, discovering solidarity that they didn't know they had. I hope this book has helped to honor their efforts.

It's possible that this is just another wave, one that's just crested a little higher than others, and that it, too, will fade and fall away, as the billionaires and the radical Right seek to denigrate work and destroy unions. It's every bit as much an uphill fight as it was five or ten years ago, have no doubt of that.

But, in this book, we've seen that workers are not just passive objects, battered about by forces beyond their control. They can step up, they can fight, they can win. And the seeds scattered by the wins of these past few years will bear all manner of fruit in the years to come, even though we can't begin to guess what they will be.

For the union makes us strong.

Epilogue: Reasons to Be Cheerful

The re-election of Donald Trump came despite the best efforts of most of the American labor movement. There were exceptions, most notably the Teamsters, who refused to endorse a candidate,* but by and large labor remembered Trump's strongly antilabor policies from 2017 through 2021, and didn't want to see them repeated.

The first weeks of the second Trump presidency have certainly justified that concern. Despite occasional nods in the campaign toward a pro-worker agenda, in practice Trump II is as pro-corporate and antiunion as Trump I. A coup is underway in plain sight, as Elon Musk and his teenage lackeys are taking over whole government departments. The damage already done is severe, and by the time you read this it will likely have gotten much, much worse. The basic human rights of immigrants, transgender people, women, and Black and brown people are all at risk.

For unions, in particular, there is no doubt the coming years will be rough. As of this writing, the great progress Starbucks Workers United made has stalled. It is possible the company will renege on its commitment to negotiate in good faith. The National Labor Relations Board will try to undo the many good things done in the past four years. The attacks on the Department of Education, and on any programs that even hint at supporting racial or

---

* The Teamsters didn't endorse at the national level. Most of the Teamsters' regional bodies came out for the Harris/Walz ticket, as did a great many of the union's largest locals across the country.

gender equity, could do great harm to education unions and their students. The very existence of federal employee unions—which, let's be honest, barely got a mention in this book—is imperiled. Far from helping the working class, the wide-ranging tariffs that Trump seems set to impose will likely cause severe economic hardship in this country and around the world. The Association of Flight Attendants is mourning its own as Trump's disregard of air safety sends planes into the ground.

The list goes on and on. A lot of bad stuff is happening, and more will happen. There's no getting around it.

It's at moments like these that labor's worst tendencies can rear their ugly heads. When Richard Nixon defeated Hubert Humphrey in 1968, more than a few unions found that racism was stronger than class solidarity. Nixon (this may sound familiar) thought he had the chance to build a durable political coalition by pulling white, mostly Catholic union members from the building trades and law enforcement into his orbit, offering token gestures of support for basic union rights while stoking division wherever possible.

The most visible example of this was the so-called Hard Hat Riot of May 8, 1970, when several hundred construction workers (whose headwear gave the event its name) descended upon antiwar protestors in New York City, attacking and injuring many while shouting pro-USA slogans. Construction unions had, in the late 1960s, found themselves pushed by civil rights advocates to give up their nepotistic structures to create opportunities for Black and Hispanic workers to get quality union jobs. There's little doubt that seething racial resentment underlay the violence of the Hard Hat Riot. The head of the New York Building and Construction Trades Council, Peter Brennan, took a stance so unapologetic that Nixon eventually made him Secretary of Labor.

Similarly, in the wake of the Second World War, anti-Communism became an excuse for more selfish pursuits. The 1947 Taft–Hartley

Act, which did much to weaken labor rights across the board, included a proviso that union leaders had to sign an affidavit, a declaration that they weren't Communist Party members. While labor fought Taft–Hartley tooth and nail, once it was passed more than a few union leaders used the affidavit provision to kick out rivals within their own union. Few did so with more gusto than Walter Reuther of the United Auto Workers.

Examples like these, sadly, are not hard to find. American unions are as flawed and fragile as any other institution in our democracy. Throughout our history, unions have had dark moments, done terrible things—it's true. Today, the president of the Teamsters, Sean O'Brien—who helped lead the contract campaign that secured such a powerful win at UPS—has become an apologist for the Trump administration, seemingly willing to overlook the administration's attack on immigrants, trans rights, freedom of the press, and worker protections. It's difficult to watch, and it must be especially difficult for Teamsters members who worked so hard to get him elected. It casts a shadow on all he has done, and the silence of the reform movement within his union is equally troubling.

There's a case to be made that the election of Trump, and the neofascist policies he is implementing, have rendered moot all of labor's progress documented in this book. It's possible that the past few years will be little more than a blip in time, a brief moment of excitement that proved transient, a short window of hope that proved elusive. Perhaps we will look back on those years and wonder how we ever were foolish enough to believe we could win.

But perhaps not. For there are still reasons for hope. For optimism, even. If anyone has the fortitude and the courage to take on fascism in America during Trump II, it's organized labor. The closest immediate parallel to the present moment is the period after the 2004 election. Despite widespread dislike of his domestic policies, George W. Bush wrapped himself tightly in the American flag and won re-election in the midst of an unwinnable war. He was expanding the powers of the national security state in a dramatic way, while his cronies were openly looting the government to line their own pockets. As now, progressives looked at his support among white union members and Latino voters, and worried that a permanent political realignment was underway.

The labor movement responded to this political setback in 2005 with infighting and fracturing. A group of unions led by SEIU pulled out of the AFL-CIO to start their own affiliate, called Change to Win (CTW). The dissidents openly invoked the founding of the CIO seventy years earlier and some hoped the split would ignite a similar wave of organizing and militancy. It didn't. Whatever the wishes or intentions of the people involved, CTW didn't provide the spark. Unions continued their decline. Conflict within the movement escalated, while conflict against bosses, in the form of strikes, became even more infrequent. Even when unions helped Barack Obama win a landslide victory, with strong congressional majorities, in 2008, they were unsuccessful in getting most of their key policy priorities passed. Unions bickered with each other, their energies focused inward as much as outward, and we entered the first Trump administration on our heels.

By contrast, instead of fracturing like in 2005, SEIU began 2025 by rejoining the AFL-CIO, demonstrating a commitment to unity in the face of strong threats. The House of Labor stood stronger together. Federal workers streamed into their unions as they dug in. The fights at Amazon and Delta continue to move forward, undaunted. I have to admit, at this exact moment, just two months into Trump's term, these steps don't necessarily feel like much. But they matter. They really do. Unions entered 2025 more united, aggressive, and ambitious than they have been in a long time.

The struggles we covered in this book have prepared labor to meet this moment. Organizing isn't just a thing you do. It's a skill you develop, a way of life you adopt. Hundreds of thousands of workers in the past few years have become organizers. Hundreds of thousands have learned that strikes can work, that solidarity can win, that their contributions to the struggle can make a difference.

Frito-Lay workers, teachers, and flight attendants have all learned how to fight back in the midst of crisis and catastrophe. They have learned that even when things look bleakest, when disease strikes and the economy collapses, workers who organize together can not only weather the storm but take the offensive. For so many decades, disaster has only benefited the wealthy. This was the first crisis in our lifetimes when workers won the fight. It's safe to say we're going to see a lot of crises. My hope is you'll be able to draw from this book inspiration to keep up the fight, to take on powerful interests, and win.

While that is happening, we can also have confidence that a new generation of labor leaders is going to step forth to the rescue and liberation of the old. Graduate employees are signing their first contracts with universities across the country, building their strength and flexing their muscles, ready to take on the attacks on higher education. Starbucks workers continue to strike, continue to organize new unions, continue to fight. The young organizers of the Emergency Workplace Organizing Committee are helping workers in every industry to build their power. The new generation of labor leaders has just begun to step onto the national stage. Their strength and influence will only grow, and that is all to the good.

In the meantime, unions are still innovating, finding new ways to challenge corporate dominance. Whatever our disappointments with specific leaders, the Teamsters and many other unions are investing real work into taking on Amazon. Their bold, persistent experimentation may yet bear fruit, and at least they're trying. The UAW has had to fight the Big Three automakers to hold on to the gains they have won—among other things, Stellantis tried to backtrack on reopening the Belvedere, Illinois, plant—but so far they're winning, and their Southern organizing continues. The Hollywood unions are now neck-deep in facing the challenge of

AI, but their interests are aligned and their recent experience of unparalleled unity will serve them well.

In 1943, during the darkest years of World War II, one of the ugliest strikes in American history took place. Twenty-five thousand white workers at a Packard plant in Detroit went on strike because company management had promoted three—yes, three—Black workers into supervisory positions. There was a term for this kind of action: a hate strike. American unions had agreed not to strike during the war, in return for union recognition in the defense industry. These strikers were actively hindering the American war effort again Nazism, and they were doing so in the name of racism. The UAW leadership was as appalled as you and I are, and the strike was quickly quashed, but the fact of it cannot be forgotten. It's a reminder of how low the American labor movement can go when it turns against solidarity.

Twenty years later, it was the UAW, along with the Brotherhood of Sleeping Car Porters, that provided much of the financial and logistical support of the March on Washington. The UAW pushed hard for civil rights in the 1960s and spent time and treasure to help advance freedom's cause. It's a reminder of how great labor can be.

But here's the thing; here's the reason I'm telling this story now. If you do the math and consider the law of averages, there is a near-certainty: Some the UAW members who helped support Dr. King and other civil rights leaders on that day in 1963 almost certainly *also* participated in the Packard hate strike in 1943.

What changed them from haters to freedom fighters? One of the main reasons has to be the union itself. Over twenty years of work on the factory floor, seeing the union raise their wages and protect their jobs and look out for their co-workers, and some of those workers came to see that race alone, that *hate* alone, wasn't what they wanted. They wanted community. They wanted shared purpose. They wanted solidarity.

Solidarity can change the world. It has before, and it will again. That's why, despite all the horrible things happening right now, I remain optimistic.

The American labor movement was supposed to be dead in the ground by now. If the trends of the first two decades of this century had continued, we would be. Instead, we're fighting, we're growing, and we're organizing. The heroes in this book are the reason why. Celebrating them is more important than ever.

Yes, it's going to be rough. But don't ever count the working class out. We've got the power.

Dave Kamper
Brooklyn Park, Minnesota
March 2025

Acknowledgments

No part of writing this book has filled me with more trepidation than these acknowledgements. There is a 100 percent chance that someone who deserves to be mentioned here will not be. To them, I apologize. Those that are listed here helped in countless ways but all the errors in this book are mine alone.

My research assistant for this project was Hanna Lee, from my alma mater, Gustavus Adolphus College. Hanna looked through hundreds of articles, videos, blog posts, and Facebook comments to help me find raw material for this book and analyzed them with precision, not only saving me research time but applying her considerable critical faculties to the work. Hanna was recommended to me by Gustavus professor of history Greg Kaster, who unfortunately passed away while this book was being written. This book is another example of his deep and abiding commitment to his students, present and former.

AFA president Sara Nelson not only gave me an extraordinary amount of time for our interview for this book but also has generously contributed the foreword. Too often, the people we hold up as model leaders come to disappoint us, but Sara Nelson is every bit as brilliant, passionate, and strategic as we want her to be. Her friendship is a real gift.

Ben Woodward at The New Press has been an invaluable editor, helping shape this book from the very beginning, providing encouragement and support as we went along, and showing patience on the many occasions it was necessary. I also want to thank Gia

Gonzales, Shelona Belfon, and the many other people at The New Press who helped this project along.

It was Lindsay Zafir who first passed my name on to Ben Woodward. During her time as publisher of *The Forge: A Journal of Organizing Strategy and Practice*, Lindsay was an incisive and thoughtful colleague, and our discussions on the state of organizing over the years gave me much food for thought. Similarly, Brian Kettenring, Miski Noor, Akin Olla, and the other editors, publishers, and volunteers at *The Forge* allowed me to try out ideas and put thoughts into the world with considerable freedom.

Two organizations shaped my growth as a union organizer and activist and are just as important to me now. When I was a young union member back in the 1990s it was easy to feel alone, that the whole world had given up on labor, until I stumbled onto the work of this obscure DC think-tank, the Economic Policy Institute. EPI's work demonstrated, in cold, hard fact, that unions were a good thing not just for their own members but for everyone. My commitment to the labor movement to that point was primarily moral—it *felt* right to be on the side of labor. Thanks to the stellar work of EPI's brilliant team, I realized that we also *were* right. EPI's work back then gave me confidence that unions were indeed everything I wanted them to be. I'm honored beyond words that for the last five years the folks at EPI have also been my colleagues. Out of a fear of leaving someone out, I'm not going to list their names, but every single one of you matters. I do want to mention one other thing: EPI's leadership never once asked to vet, see, or review the content of this book, even though many of the unions mentioned in these pages fund our work. I hope I have merited that trust.

Thanks also to my comrades in our staff union, EPI United, who have at times shown me extraordinary patience and given me their confidence. I'm also proudly a member of the NewsGuild and the National Writers Union.

The other organization that molded me as a unionist in my early days was Labor Notes. Their book, *Democracy Is Power*, helped shape my philosophy of unionism, and their fighting spirit has sustained me through many difficult times. Their help has been more personal, too. Dan DiMaggio of Labor Notes spotted something I'd written in early 2016 and gave me my first break, spreading my work to a much broader audience than I would have gotten on my own, opening doors for me I never even knew existed. Their constant encouragement, and the standard of fiery solidarity and journalistic integrity they set is one I hope to have met in this book. If you have read this far into the Acknowledgements section of this book, now is a great time to put this down and send them a donation. In addition to Dan DiMaggio above, special appreciation to Al Bradbury, Luis Feliz Leon, Joe Demanuelle-Hall, Sarah Hughes, Courtney Smith, and Natascha Elena Uhlmann, but everyone at Labor Notes is awesome even if I didn't mention them here. Register now for their 2026 conference in Chicago! I'll be volunteering at the registration desk and would love to say hi.

A great many wonderful union members and leaders gave of their time and spirit to talk to me for this book. In addition to many who spoke to me off the record, I want to thank the following for speaking to me and also helping me connect with others who I was able to talk to: Chantel Mendenhall, Mark Benaka, Jason Davis, Pleasant Desch, Esther Fanning, Brent Hall, Shane Nichols, Cheri Renfro, Brad Schmidt, and Bruni Torres of BCTGM; Eden Mc-Causlin and Linda Perales of the Chicago Teachers Union; Jasmine Leli of Starbucks Workers United; Margaret Czerwienski and Amulya Mandava of the Harvard Graduate Student Union; Cal Mergendahl and Noah Wexler of the GLU at the University of Minnesota; Caleb Andrews of the TRU at Johns Hopkins; Promise Li of GSU at Princeton; and Sasha Brietzke, Logan Mann, and Rendi Rogers of GOLD-UE at Dartmouth.

I've been incredibly fortunate, over the last decade and more, to have the well-timed and unselfish support of people in and around the labor movement who thought the things I was writing were valuable, and who put opportunities my way that I otherwise would not have had. Among others, Micah Uetricht and Shawn Gude at *Jacobin*, along with their other talented staff, gave me tremendous freedom to write things that I now look back on and consider perhaps a trifle foolish. I hope I am able to pay such kindnesses forward, as there are a great many talented thinkers and writers in labor today who could use the same boosts I got.

The students in my 2024 Labor History class at the Union Leadership and Activism (ULA) program at the University of Massachusetts Amherst may not have understood they were a sounding board for some of the ideas in this book, but our wonderful discussions had a real impact on what's in here. The ULA program staff and my fellow faculty, including Courtney Derwinski, Sierra Dickey, Clare Hammonds, Tom Juravich, Jasmine Kerrissey, Gordon Lafer, Laura Liu, Nellie Taylor, and Eve Weinbaum, were wonderful colleagues who made the work a pleasure.

I've had the great pleasure, during this time, to serve as an organizer with the Emergency Workplace Organizing Committee. It is possible I have underplayed EWOC's role in this book, because I don't know that I'm able to see its impact with objectivity, but everyone involved with EWOC is doing amazing work and their story deserves to be told far and wide. Special thanks to Patrick Cale, Megan Svoboda, Dawn Tefft, and Daphna Thier.

One of the best American historians in the country, Professor Robert M. Owens of Wichita State University, generously reviewed the manuscript and made many useful suggestions.

A great many other people gave me time and encouragement, or shared their expertise, as this project progressed, perhaps without even knowing it, including Drew Astolfi, Eric Blanc, Chris Bohner, Erica Clemmons Dean, Arielle Edelman McHenry, Susan Kang, Connor Lewis, Erik Loomis, Meg Luger-Nikolai, Larry

Nelson, Alyssa Picard, Will Roberts, Johanna Schussler, and Gabriel Winant. I thank Kelly Goodman for use of her unpublished doctoral dissertation.

Our cats—Mr. Pickles, Simon Sparklepants, Laverne, Shirley, and Inspector Waffles—demonstrated their approval of this project by never once throwing up on my computer.

Above all, always above all, the love of my life, my bride, Joanne Biederman Kamper, deserves thanks. She's the only person I know who I'm willing to *admit* is smarter than me, and her feedback, suggestions, and thoughts were on point and valuable. She has always given full support to my efforts to establish myself as a writer, and without her buttressing my fragile ego, I never would have had the courage. I am lucky beyond measure to have her by my side. Love you, Jojobean.

Brooklyn Park, Minnesota, March 2025

Notes

A note on references:
Unless otherwise cited, data on the number of union members in a state, occupation, or industry, or on the density of union membership, comes from the Union Membership and Coverage Database maintained by Barry Hirsch, David Macpherson, and William Even, *https://unionstats.com/*. This is an invaluable resource that is of great value to the movement.

Also, unless I cite otherwise, quotes from people in this book come from interviews I did with them in 2023 or 2024.

Introduction

1. Josh Bivens, "The Post-Pandemic Recovery Is an Economic Policy Success Story," *Working Economics Blog*, Economic Policy Institute, October 1, 2024, www.epi.org/blog.

2. Naomi Klein, *The Shock Doctrine: The Rise of Disaster Capitalism*, 1st ed. (New York: Metropolitan Books/Henry Holt, 2007).

1. Worked to the Bone

1. James Gray Pope, "How American Workers Lost the Right to Strike, and Other Tales," *Michigan Law Review* 103, no. 3 (December 2004).

2. See, for example, Perea, "The Echoes of Slavery: Recognizing the Racist Origins of the Agricultural and Domestic Worker Exclusion from the National Labor Relations Act."

3. For a good overview of this in the context of the whole of labor history, see Loomis, *A History of America in Ten Strikes*.

4. McGowan, "Industrializing the Land of Lono: Sugar Plantation Managers and Workers in Hawaii, 1900–1920."

5. Brenner, Day, and Ness, *The Encyclopedia of Strikes in American History*.

6. Dan DiMaggio, "'It Feels Like We Started a Movement': Despite Mixed Results in Frito-Lay Strike, Workers Proud They Stood Up," Labor Notes (October 25 2021). labornotes.org/blogs.

7. There's a long and complicated history attached to the UFW. For more, you could start with Ross and United Farm Workers of America, *Conquering Goliath: Cesar Chavez at the Beginning*; and Bardacke, *Trampling Out the Vintage: Cesar Chavez and the Two Souls of the United Farm Workers*.

8. Peter J. Rachleff, *Hard-Pressed in the Heartland: The Hormel Strike and the Future of the Labor Movement,* 1st ed. (Boston, MA: South End Press, 1993).

9. Noam Scheiber, "Kellogg Workers Ratify a Revised Contract After Being on Strike Since October," *New York Times,* December 21, 2021.

2. Running Out of Adults in the Classroom

1. American Federation of Teachers, "Road Map to Safely Reopening Our Schools," February 2021, www.aft.org/sites/default/files/media/documents/2022 /aft-reopen-schools-one-pager.

2. David Weigel and Shelby Talcott, "Mike Pompeo: 'The Most Dangerous Person in the World Is Randi Weingarten,'" *Semafor,* May 21, 2022, www .semafor.com/article/11/21/2022/mike-pompeo-2024-trump.

3. For more details on the shortcomings in Oster's methodology, see Rachel M. Cohen, "Why Reopening Schools Has Become the Most Fraught Debate of the Pandemic," *American Prospect,* October 28, 2020.

4. Bryan Walsh, "The Racial Divide in Returning to the Classroom," *Axios,* February 6, 2021.

5. For a rundown of many of these criticisms and their inaccuracy, see Madison Czopek, "Here's What AFT's Randi Weingarten Said About Reopening Schools During COVID-19," *Politifact,* May 2, 2023, www.politifact.com /article.

6. The best overview of the early years of these unions is Marjorie Murphy, *Blackboard Unions: The AFT and the NEA, 1900–1980* (Ithaca, NY: Cornell University Press, 1990).

7. Paul M. Secunda, "The Wisconsin Public-Sector Labor Dispute of 2011," *ABA Journal of Labor and Employment Law* 27, no. 293 (2012).

8. Kelly Goodman, "Tax the Rich: Teachers' Long Campaign to Fund Public Schools" (Yale University, 2021), 172 *et seq.*

9. Secunda, "The Wisconsin Public-Sector Labor Dispute of 2011."

10. Alana Samuels, "Is This the End of Public-Sector Unions in America?" *The Atlantic,* June 27, 2018.

11. Jackson Potter, "The Caucus of Rank-and-File Educators Changed American Teachers Unionism," *Jacobin,* June 7, 2023, jacobin.com.

12. For an overview of the Red for Ed strikes, see Eric Blanc, *Red State Revolt: the Teachers' Strike Wave and Working-Class Politics,* Jacobin series (London, New York: Verso, 2019).

13. Barbara Madeloni, "As Omicron Rages, Teachers and Students Fight for Safety Measures in Chicago and Elsewhere," Labor Notes, January 13, 2022, labornotes.org.

14. Mara Klecker and Ryan Faircloth, "Minneapolis Teachers Walk Picket Lines as Strike Begins," *Minnesota Star-Tribune,* March 8, 2022, www .startribune.com/minneapolis-teachers-union-strike-begins-class-will-be-in -session-in-st-paul.

15. This is a little-told, fascinating story, covered in great detail in Ariel Branz, *Colors of Solidarity*, podcast audio, 2024.

16. Greta Callahan and Shaun Laden, "Minneapolis Educators Just Showed the Country How to Strike and Win," interview by Eric Blanc, *Jacobin*, March 29, 2022, jacobin.com/2022/03/minneapolis-teachers-mft-strike-union-reform.

17. Jon Peltz, "In Los Angeles, 60,000 Education Workers Just Went on Strike and Won Big," *Jacobin*, March 28, 2023, jacobin.com/2023/03/los-angeles-education-workers-strike-lausd-utla-seiu-local-99.

18. Courtney E. Martin, "Teachers Are Striking for More Than Just Pay Raises," *Vox*, July 16, 2023, www.vox.com/2023/7/16/23792870/teacher-strike-oakland-union-common-good-bargaining.

19. For the full story, see Nelson Lichtenstein, *The Most Dangerous Man in Detroit: Walter Reuther and the Fate of American Labor* (New York: Basic Books, 1995).

3. The Runway Not Taken

1. Niraj Chokshi, "Flight Attendants and Pilots Ask, 'Is It OK to Keep Working?'" *New York Times*, April 12, 2020.

2. See, for example, Ruth Milkman, *Women, Work, and Protest: a Century of U.S. Women's Labor History* (London, New York: Routledge & Kegan Paul, 1987).

3. Sara Nelson, "Japan Aircraft Collision Demonstrates How Safety Protocols Work," interview by A. Martinez, *NPR Morning Edition*, January 4, 2024, www.npr.org.

4. Nell McShane Wulfhart, *The Great Stewardess Rebellion: How Women Launched a Workplace Rebellion at 30,000 feet*, 1st ed. (New York: Doubleday, 2022).

5. Dave Kamper, "Union Democracy Is a Value, Not a Strategy," *Jacobin*, January 31, 2024, jacobin.com/2024/01/union-democracy-organizing-militancy-strategy.

6. See, for example, Robert Kuttner, "A Union of Their Own," *Prospect*, September 28, 2023, prospect.org/labor/2023-09-28-union-of-their-own-flight-attendants.

7. What follows comes primarily from my interviews with Sara Nelson, but much of this story was also covered in Claire Bushey, "Sara Nelson: the Union Boss Fighting to 'Put Workers First,'" *Financial Times*, October 1, 2020, www.ft.com.

8. Sara Nelson, *COVID-19 Airline Relief Starts with Workers* (2020).

9. William R. Emmons and Drew Dahl, "Was the Paycheck Protection Program Effective?" Federal Reserve Bank of St. Louis, July 6, 2022, www.stlouisfed.org/publications/regional-economist.

10. Sally French and Sam Kemmis, "Travel Inflation Report: April 2024," *NerdWallet*, April 23, 2024, www.nerdwallet.com/article/travel/travel-price-tracker.

11. Tacey Rychter, "Flight Attendants' Hellish Summer: 'I Don't Even

Feel Like a Human,'" *New York Times,* August 26, 2021, www.nytimes.com /2021/08/26/travel/flight-attendant-burnout.

12. Neil Vigdor, "Passenger Arrives Taped to a Seat and Is Charged with Assaulting Flight Attendants," *New York Times,* August 3, 2021, www.nytimes .com/2021/08/03/business/max-berry-frontier-airlines-flight-attendant-assault.

13. Vimal Patel, "Women Gets 15 Months in Prison for Punching Flight Attendant in the Face," *New York Times,* May 28, 2022, www.nytimes .com/2022/06/01/us/flight-attendant-punched-sentencing.

14. Ruthy Munoz, "A Year of Pandemic Flying Exacts Heavy Toll on Flight Crews: Union Boss," *Skift,* February 23, 2021, skift.com.

15. For a fuller account of Operation Dixie, see Barbara S. Griffith, *The Crisis of American Labor: Operation Dixie and the Defeat of the CIO* (Philadelphia: Temple University Press, 1988).

16. The story of Warrior Met is one of many that deserves far more attention than this book is able to devote to it. The labor journalist Kim Kelly covered the strike from the beginning. Her piece on the end of the strike is at Kim Kelly, "Why the Warrior Met Strike Is Ending," *The Nation,* February 20, 2023, www.thenation.com/article/activism/warrior-met-strike-union.

17. See Chandra Childers, *Rooted in Racism and Exploitation: the Failed Southern Economic Development Model,* Economic Policy Institute, October 11, 2023, www.epi.org.

18. A good source on the 2018–19 strike wave is Eric Blanc, *Red State Revolt: the Teachers' Strike Wave and Working-Class Politics,* Jacobin series (London, New York: Verso, 2019).

19. West Virginia Department of Education, Professional Salary Schedules (Summary) 24 (2024).

20. The leaders of the strike talk about it in great detail in this video: Labor Notes, "Panel: Stories from the West Virginia Teachers Strike" (2018), www .facebook.com/watch/live.

Part II: The Children of 2008

1. Under circumstances that actually do seem sort of suspicious. See Michael Parenti, "The Wonderful Life and Strange Death of Walter Reuther," *CovertAction,* Fall 1995.

2. Aurelia Glass, "What You Need to Know About Gen Z's Support for Unions," Center for American Progress, August 9, 2023, www .americanprogress.org/article.

3. Dave Kamper, "What's Fueling the Grad Worker Upsurge?" Labor Notes, March 22, 2023, labornotes.org.

4. Solidarity Takes Down the Whale

1. Judith Wellman, *Grass Roots Reform in the Burned-over District of Upstate New York: Religion, Abolitionism, and Democracy,* Studies in African American

History and Culture (New York: Garland Publishing, 2000), publisher description, www.loc.gov/catdir/enhancements/fy0652/00042948-d.html.

2. The story is very similar to the story of Pittsburgh, as told in Gabriel Winant, *The Next Shift: the Fall of Industry and the Rise of Health Care in Rust Belt America* (Cambridge, MA: Harvard University Press, 2021).

3. Anna Blatto, *A City Divided: a Brief History of Segregation in Buffalo*, Partnership for the Public Good (Partnership for the Public Good, April 2018), ppgbuffalo.org/files/documents/data-demographics-history.

4. Quoted in Heather Wood Rudolph, "Interview Insider: How to Get Hired at Starbucks," *Cosmopolitan*, September 11, 2014, www.cosmopolitan.com/career/interviews/a30807/interview-insider-starbucks-career-jobs.

5. Colin Marshall, "The First Starbucks Coffee Shop, Seattle—a History of Cities in 50 Buildings, Day 36," *The Guardian*, May 14, 2015.

6. Noam Scheiber, "Starbucks Falls Short After Pledging Better Labor Practices," *New York Times*, September 23, 2015.

7. Nelson Lichtenstein and Judith Stein, *A Fabulous Failure: the Clinton Presidency and the Transformation of American Capitalism*, Politics and Society in Modern America (Princeton: Princeton University Press, 2023).

8. Ben Mathis-Lilley, "If Leaked List Is Accurate, Hillary's Cabinet Choices Would Have Enraged the Democratic Left," *Slate*, January 10, 2017, slate.com/news-and-politics/2017/01/hillary-cabinet-plans-leaked-sheryl-sandberg-at-treasury-starbucks-ceo-at-labor.html.

9. Chris Isidore, "Starbucks Workers at Buffalo Store Vote to Unionize," *CNN Business*, December 9, 2021, edition.cnn.com/2021/12/09/business/starbucks-union-vote/index.html.

10. The classic work on the close connections between where and how workers lived, and the unions they built, is Lizabeth Cohen, *Making a New Deal: Industrial Workers in Chicago, 1919–1939* (Cambridge, England; New York: Cambridge University Press, 1990).

11. Alex N. Press, "Occupy Wall Street Made Me a Socialist," *Jacobin*, September 21, 2021, jacobin.com/2021/09/occupy-wall-street-anniversary-boston-dewey-square-99-percent.

12. Gabriel Winant, "A New Political Identity," *Dissent*, September 17, 2021, www.dissentmagazine.org/online_articles.

13. Noah Lanard, "Howard Schultz Came Out of Retirement to Destroy Starbucks' Union—and His Legacy," *Mother Jones*, March 2023, www.motherjones.com/politics/2023/03/howard-schultz-starbucks-union-busting-buffalo-brooklyn. The Memphis Seven firings were determined to be illegal and the workers won reinstatement.

14. The most complete data can be found at "Current Starbucks Statistics," Union Election Data, 2024, unionelections.org/data/starbucks.

15. Leonard C. Scott, Handwritten Notes on Counter-Union Campaigns, 1978, September 23, 1978; Leonard Scott, Union-Prevention and Counter-Union Campaign Consulting Files #6474, Kheel Center for Labor-Management Documentation and Archives, Cornell University Library. Emphasis added.

16. Jenny Brown, "Starbucks Workers Win Breakthrough Promise of Real Negotiations," Labor Notes, February 29, 2024.

17. Frank Swoboda, "Wal-Mart Ends Meat-Cutting Jobs," *Washington Post,* March 3, 2000.

18. Christian Smalls and Jaz Brisack, "We're Organizing Unions at Amazon and Starbucks. We Won't Back Down," Interview by Daniel Denvir, *Jacobin,* May 2022, jacobin.com/2022/05/amazon-starbucks-labor-union-busting-nlrb.

19. See, for example, Jack Fiorito, Irene Padavic, and Zachary A. Russell, "Union Beliefs and Activism: a Research Note," *Journal of Labor Research* 35 (2014).

20. Suhauna Hussain, "These L.A. Strippers Won a Union. But the Dance Isn't Over," *Los Angeles Times,* October 5, 2023.

21. The best analysis of the kind of volunteer-led organizing exemplified by EWOC can be found in Eric Blanc, *We Are the Union: How Worker-to-Worker Organizing Is Revitalizing Labor and Winning Big,* 1st ed. (Oakland: University of California Press, 2022).

22. Daisy Pitkin, *On the Line: a Story of Class, Solidarity, and Two Women's Epic Fight to Build a Union,* 1st ed. (Chapel Hill, NC: Algonquin Books of Chapel Hill, 2022).

23. Lanard, "Howard Schultz Came Out of Retirement to Destroy Starbucks' Union—and His Legacy."

24. Brown, "Starbucks Workers Win Breakthrough Promise of Real Negotiations."

5. Organizing the Ivy League

1. U.S. Bureau of Labor Statistics, Work Stoppages Data, www.bls.gov/web/wkstp/monthly-listing.xlsx.

2. While there is now an educational travel organization called Road Scholar, the term has been around for many years to refer to adjunct faculty who spend much of their time driving between campuses, and I'm not referring to the travel company. See, for example, Chad Christensen, "The Employment of Part-Time Faculty at Community Colleges," *New Directions for Higher Education* 143 (2008).

3. See, for example, Jeremy Young, "Christopher Rufo's Alarming and Deceptive Crusade Against Public Universities," *Time,* August 10, 2023.

4. National Labor Relations Board, "The Leland Stanford Junior University, 214 N.L.R.B. 621," ed. National Labor Relations Board, 1974.

5. Michael Sainato, "Amazon Could Run Out of Workers in U.S. in Two Years, Internal Memo Suggests," *The Guardian,* June 22, 2022.

6. See, for example, Katie Roiphe, "Why Professors Should Never Have Affairs with Their Students," *Slate,* May 21, 2015. The mere fact that Roiphe had to treat this idea as something other than self-evident is a sign of how deeply corrupted the system is.

7. Tilly R. Robinson, "Embattled Harvard Professor John Comaroff Retires Without Emeritus Status," *Harvard Crimson,* August 2, 2024.

8. Stuart Anderson, "International Students Remain a Primary Source of U.S. Tech Talent," *Forbes,* August 19, 2021.

9. See also Kate Bronfenbrenner, *Organizing to Win: New Research on Union Strategies* (Ithaca, NY: ILR Press, 1998).

6. The New Flints

1. There are numerous accounts of the Flint Sit-Down. For the most you-are-there thrills, consult Mary Heaton Vorse, *Labor's New Millions* (New York: Modern Age Books, 1938).

2. Many others have made this point. See, for example, Kim Moody, "Labor's New Terrain: Working On the Supply Chain Gang," Labor Notes, June 5, 2018, www.labornotes.org.

3. Camila Domonoske, "Why Car Prices Are Still So High—and Why They Are Unlikely to Fall Anytime Soon," National Public Radio, 2023.

4. See Loomis, 54–55.

5. For a full description of this, see Aaron Gordon, "'The Worst and Most Egregious Attendance Policy' Is Pushing Railroad Workers to the Brink," *Vice,* April 5, 2022, www.vice.com/en/article.

6. Joseph Anthony McCartin, *Collision Course: Ronald Reagan, the Air Traffic Controllers, and the Strike That Changed America* (New York: Oxford University Press, 2011).

7. Peter J. Rachleff, *Hard-Pressed in the Heartland: The Hormel Strike and the Future of the Labor Movement,* 1st ed. (Boston, MA: South End Press, 1993). There was also a moving documentary, *American Dream,* released in the early 1990s.

8. Ryan Cooper, "For Workers, Unions and Public Pressure Get the Goods," *American Prospect,* June 26, 2023, prospect.org/labor/2023-06 -26-workers-rail-unions-public-pressure.

9. What follows in the next few paragraphs is taken in large part from my article on the Shakopee Prime Day strike; see Dave Kamper, "'We're Workers, Not Robots,'" *Jacobin,* July 16, 2019, jacobin.com/2019/07 /amazon-strike-prime-day-shakopee-fulfillment-center.

10. Strategic Organizing Center, *In Denial: Amazon's Continuing Failure to Fix Its Injury Crisis,* April 2023, warehouseworkers.org/wp-content /uploads/2023/04/SOC_In-Denial_Amazon-Injury-Report-April-2023.pdf.

11. Lauren Kaori Gurley and Caroline O'Donovan, "Amazon Prime Day Causes Workplace Injuries, Senate Probe Finds," *Washington Post,* July 16, 2024, www.washingtonpost.com/business/2024/07/16 /bernie-sanders-amazon-investigation.

12. Alex N. Press, "Amazon Waged a Brutal Anti-Union Campaign. Unsurprisingly, They Won," *Jacobin,* April 9, 2021, jacobin.com/2021/04 /amazon-bessemer-union-drive-vote-nlrb.

13. This section relies heavily on the brilliant work of Catherine Rios and David Witwer, *Murder in the Garment District,* which is, in an outstanding

example of brand synergy, also published by The New Press, which is publishing this book.

14. Tracy Samilton, "Fiat Chrysler Will Plead to Criminal Charge in UAW Corruption Scandal," Michigan Public, January 28, 2021, www.michiganpublic.org/law.

15. Luis Feliz Leon, "Inside the Teamsters' Historic Contract at UPS," *American Prospect*, July 25, 2023, prospect.org/labor.

16. Ben Douglass and Luigi Morris, "10 Reasons UPS Workers Are Voting 'No' on the Tentative Agreement," *Left Voice*, August 11, 2023, www.leftvoice.org.

7. Somehow Striking Feels Good in a Place Like This

1. Shera Avi-Yonah and Andrea Salcedo, "Ronald Reagan Led an Actors Strike Decades Before His U.S. Presidency," *Washington Post*, July 14, 2023.

2. Veena Dubal and Juliet B. Schor, "Gig Workers Are Employees. Start Treating Them That Way," *New York Times*, January 18, 2021, www.nytimes.com/2021/01/18/opinion/proposition-22-california-biden.html.

3. Luke Goldstein, "Massachusetts Ballot Measure Criticized for Creating Gig Worker 'Company Unions,'" *American Prospect*, September 23, 2024, prospect.org/labor.

4. Hamilton Nolan, *The Hammer: Power, Inequality, and the Struggle for the Soul of Labor*, 1st ed. (New York: Hachette Books, 2024).

5. Ronald Blum, "Minor Leaguers Form Union, 17 Days After Organizing Began," *AP News*, September 14, 2022, apnews.com/article.

6. Cynthia Littleton, "Revisting the 1980s SAG-AFTRA Strike with 'MASH' Stars, an Emmy Boycott and All-Night Negotiating Sessions: 'We're Going to Strike Like Hell,'" *Variety*, September 1, 2023, variety.com/2023/biz/news/sag-actors-strike-1980-similarities-differences.

7. Rick Perlstein, *Reaganland: America's Right Turn 1976–1980* (New York: Simon & Schuster, 2020).

8. Dave McNary, "Protests Filed over SAG-AFTRA's Gabrielle Carteris Election Win," *Page Six*, September 4, 2019, pagesix.com; variety.com.

9. David Robb, "SAG-AFTRA Election Turns Ugly as Allegations and Threats of Lawsuits Fly Between Feuding Camps," *Deadline*, August 16, 2021, deadline.com.

10. Joy Press, "Meet the Writers Strike's Secret Weapon: Hollywood Teamster Boss Lindsay Dougherty," *Variety Fair*, May 17, 2023, www.vanityfair.com/hollywood. This article repeats an all-too-common error by reporters—referring to Dougherty as a "boss" even though she was elected to her position by a membership vote.

11. Sam Luebke and Jennifer Luff, "Organizing: A Secret History," *Labor History* 44, no. 4 (2003).

12. Shaan Sharma, "UNITY: 2023 Letter to SAG-AFTRA L.A. Members," *Medium*, September 4, 2023, medium.com/@coalitionoflight.

13. See, for example, Howard A. Rodman and Alex O'Keefe, "With Their Five-Month Strike, Hollywood Writers Scored a Historic Victory," Interview by Barry Eidlin, *Jacobin,* November 21, 2023, jacobin.com.

8. It Doesn't Have to Be This Way

1. Lordstown was just one of many strikes and labor actions that demonstrated workers' dissatisfaction with the status quo. See the essays in Aaron Brenner, Robert Brenner, and Calvin Winslow, *Rebel Rank and File: Labor Militancy and Revolt from Below During the Long 1970s* (London, New York: Verso, 2010).

2. Jonah Furman, "Auto Workers to Vote on Direct Elections for Officers," Labor Notes, September 27, 2021, labornotes.org/2021/09/auto-workers-vote-direct-electi.

3. One of the deans of this school of campaign research is Tom Juravich, whose essay, Tom Juravich, "Beating Global Capital: A Framework and Method for Union Strategic Corporate Rsearch and Campaigns," in *Global Unions: Challenging Global Capital Through Cross-Border Campaigns,* ed. Kate Bronfenbrenner (Ithaca, NY : Cornell University Press, 2007), is one of the touchstones of the field. Lots of other people have written about contract campaigns. The reason Juravich matters here is that the person Shawn Fain appointed as his chief of staff when he took office, Chris Brooks, was a student of Juravich's.

4. Shawn Fain, "Exclusive: UAW President Shawn Fain on How the Auto Workers Won and What's Next," *In These Times,* November 7, 2023, inthesetimes.com/article/exclusive-interview-uaw-president-shawn-fain.

5. See, for example, "UAW's President Shawn Fain Makes Gains in Strike Talks, but Some Wonder: Has He Reached Too Far?" *CBS News Detroit,* October 23, 2023, www.cbsnews.com/detroit/news.

6. Luis Feliz Leon and Jane Slaughter, "Auto Workers Strike Plants at All Three of the Big 3," Labor Notes, September 15, 2023, labornotes.org. Feliz Leon's coverage of the lead-up to the strike and the strike itself was exemplary, influencing mainstream media coverage of the strike and setting a high standard for labor reporting. One of the by-products of the resurgence of unions is that Labor Notes, always a scrappy, small organization, saw a significant increase in subscriptions and donations, and was able to hire more full-time journalists like Feliz Leon, who then had the time to dive deeply into strikes and organizing drives.

7. Keith Brower Brown, "Auto Workers Escalate: Surprise Strike at Massive Kentucky Ford Truck Plant," Labor Notes, October 11, 2023, labornotes.org.

Bibliography

Introduction

Bivens, Josh. "The Post-Pandemic Recovery Is an Economic Policy Success Story." *Working Economics Blog,* Economic Policy Institute, October 1, 2024, www.epi.org/blog.

Klein, Naomi. *The Shock Doctrine: The Rise of Disaster Capitalism.* 1st ed. New York: Metropolitan Books/Henry Holt, 2007.

1. Worked to the Bone

Bardacke, Frank, ed. *Trampling out the Vintage: Cesar Chavez and the Two Souls of the United Farm Workers.* Paperback edition. London: Verso, 2012.

Brenner, Aaron, Benjamin Day, and Immanuel Ness. *The Encyclopedia of Strikes in American History.* Armonk, NY: M.E. Sharpe, 2009.

DiMaggio, Dan. "'It Feels Like We Started a Movement': Despite Mixed Results in Frito-Lay Strike, Workers Proud They Stood Up." Labor Notes, October 25, 2021. labornotes.org/blogs/2021/10.

Loomis, Erik. *A History of America in Ten Strikes.* New York: The New Press, 2018.

McGowan, William P. "Industrializing the Land of Lono: Sugar Plantation Managers and Workers in Hawaii, 1900–1920." *Agircultural History* 69, no. 2 (1995).

Perea, Juan F. "The Echoes of Slavery: Recognizing the Racist Origins of the Agricultural and Domestic Worker Exclusion from the National Labor Relations Act." *Ohio State Law Journal* 72, no. 1 (2011).

Pope, James Gray. "How American Workers Lost the Right to Strike, and Other Tales." *Michigan Law Review* 103, no. 3 (December 2004): 518–53.

Rachleff, Peter J. *Hard-Pressed in the Heartland: the Hormel Strike and the Future of the Labor Movement.* 1st ed. Boston, MA: South End Press, 1993.

Ross, Fred, and United Farm Workers of America. *Conquering Goliath: Cesar Chavez at the Beginning.* 1st ed. Keene, CA: United Farm Workers/Distributed by El Taller Grafico, 1989.

Scheiber, Noam. "Kellogg Workers Ratify a Revised Contract After Being on Strike Since October." *New York Times,* December 21 2021.

2. Running Out of Adults in the Classroom

American Federation of Teachers. "Road Map to Safely Reopening Our Schools." February 2021. www.aft.org/sites/default/files/media /documents.

Blanc, Eric. *Red State Revolt: the Teachers' Strike Wave and Working-Class Politics.* Jacobin Series. London, New York: Verso, 2019.

Branz, Ariel. *Colors of Solidarity.* Podcast audio, 2024.

Callahan, Greta, and Shaun Laden. "Minneapolis Educators Just Showed the Country How to Strike and Win." By Eric Blanc. *Jacobin,* March 29, 2022. jacobin.com.

Cohen, Rachel M. "Why Reopening Schools Has Become the Most Fraught Debate of the Pandemic." *American Prospect,* October 28, 2020.

Czopek, Madison. "Here's What AFT's Randi Weingarten Said About Reopening Schools During Covid-19." *Politifact,* May 2, 2023. www .politifact.com/article.

Goodman, Kelly. "Tax the Rich: Teachers' Long Campaign to Fund Public Schools." Yale University, 2021.

Klecker, Mara, and Ryan Faircloth. "Minneapolis Teachers Walk Picket Lines as Strike Begins." *Minnesota Star-Tribune,* March 8, 2022. www .startribune.com/minneapolis-teachers-union-strike-begins-class-will-be-in -session-in-st-paul.

Lichtenstein, Nelson. *The Most Dangerous Man in Detroit: Walter Reuther and the Fate of American Labor.* New York, NY: Basic Books, 1995.

Madeloni, Barbara. "As Omicron Rages, Teachers and Students Fight for Safety Measures in Chicago and Elsewhere." Labor Notes, January 13, 2022. labornotes.org.

Martin, Courtney E. "Teachers Are Striking for More Than Just Pay Raises." *Vox,* July 16 2023. www.vox.com/2023/7/16/23792870/teacher -strike-oakland-union-common-good-bargaining.

Murphy, Marjorie. *Blackboard Unions: the AFT and the NEA, 1900–1980.* Ithaca, NY: Cornell University Press, 1990.

Peltz, Jon. "In Los Angeles, 60,000 Education Workers Just Went on Strike and Won Big." *Jacobin,* March 28, 2023. jacobin.com/2023/03 /los-angeles-education-workers-strike-lausd-utla-seiu-local-99.

Potter, Jackson. "The Caucus of Rank-and-File Educators Changed American Teachers Unionism." Jacobin, June 7, 2023. jacobin.com/2023/06 /core-caucus-of-rank-and-file-educators-chicago-teachers-unionism.

Samuels, Alana. "Is This the End of Public-Sector Unions in America?" *The Atlantic,* June 27, 2018.

Secunda, Paul M. "The Wisconsin Public-Sector Labor Dispute of 2011." *ABA Journal of Labor and Employment Law* 27, no. 293 (2012): 293–305.

Walsh, Bryan. "The Racial Divide in Returning to the Classroom." *Axios,* February 6, 2021.

Weigel, David, and Shelby Talcott. "Mike Pompeo: 'The Most Dangerous

Person in the World Is Randi Weingarten.'" *Semafor,* May 21, 2022. www
.semafor.com/article.

3. The Runway Not Taken

Blanc, Eric. *Red State Revolt: the Teachers' Strike Wave and Working-Class Politics.* Jacobin Series. London, New York: Verso, 2019.

Bushey, Claire. "Sara Nelson: the Union Boss Fighting to 'Put Workers First.'"
Financial Times, October 1, 2020. www.ft.com.

Childers, Chandra. *Rooted in Racism and Exploitation: the Failed Southern
Economic Development Model.* Economic Policy Institute, October 11, 2023.
www.epi.org/publication.

Chokshi, Niraj. "Flight Attendants and Pilots Ask, 'Is It OK to Keep Working?'" *New York Times,* April 12, 2020.

Emmons, William R., and Drew Dahl. "Was the Paycheck Protection Program
Effective?" Federal Reserve Bank of St. Louis, July 6, 2022. www.stlouisfed
.org/publications/regional-economist.

French, Sally, and Sam Kemmis. "Travel Inflation Report: April 2024." *Nerd-
Wallet,* April 23, 2024. www.nerdwallet.com/article/travel/travel-price-tracker.

Griffith, Barbara S. *The Crisis of American Labor: Operation Dixie and the Defeat of the CIO.* Philadelphia: Temple University Press, 1988.

Kamper, Dave. "Union Democracy Is a Value, Not a Strategy." *Jacobin,* January 31,
2004. jacobin.com/2024/01/union-democracy-organizing-militancy-strategy.

Kelly, Kim. "Why the Warrior Met Strike Is Ending." *The Nation,* February
20, 2023. www.thenation.com/article/activism/warrior-met-strike-union.

Kuttner, Robert. "A Union of Their Own." *American Prospect,* September 28,
2023. *prospect.org/labor.*

Labor Notes. "Panel: Stories from the West Virginia Teachers Strike." 2018. https://
www.facebook.com/watch/live/?ref=watch_permalink&v=10156285060014686.

Martinez, A. "Japan Aircraft Collision Demonstrates How Safety Protocols
Work." *Morning Edition,* January 4, 2024. www.npr.org.

McShane Wulfhart, Nell. *The Great Stewardess Rebellion: How Women
Launched a Workplace Rebellion at 30,000 Feet.* 1st ed. New York: Doubleday, 2022.

Milkman, Ruth. *Women, Work, and Protest: a Century of U.S. Women's Labor
History.* London, New York: Routledge & Kegan Paul, 1987.

Munoz, Ruthy. "A Year of Pandemic Flying Exacts Heavy Toll on Flight
Crews: Union Boss." *Skift,* February 23, 2021. skift.com.

Nolan, Hamilton. "Sara Nelson: Our Airline Relief Bill Is a Template for
Rescuing Workers Instead of Bailing Out Execs." *In These Times,* March 19,
2020.

Nolan, Hamilton. "How the Mighty Culinary Union Survived the Apocalypse." *In These Times,* December 15, 2021. inthesetimes.com/article/vegas
-culinary-union-pandemic-shutdown-workers.

Patel, Vimal. "Women Gets 15 Months in Prison for Punching Flight Attendant in the Face." *New York Times,* May 28, 2022. www.nytimes.com.

Rychter, Tacey. "Flight Attendants' Hellish Summer: 'I Don't Even Feel Like a Human.'" *New York Times,* August 26, 2021. www.nytimes.com /2021/08/26/travel/flight-attendant-burnout.html.

Vigdor, Neil. "Passenger Arrives Taped to a Seat and Is Charged with Assaulting Flight Attendants." *New York Times,* August 3, 2021. www.nytimes.com/2021 /08/03/business/max-berry-frontier-airlines-flight-attendant-assault.

West Virginia Department of Education. *Professional Salary Schedules (Summary)* 24, 2024.

Part II: The Children of 2008

Glass, Aurelia. "What You Need to Know About Gen Z's Support for Unions." *American Progress.* www.americanprogress.org/article.

Kamper, Dave. "What's Fueling the Grad Worker Upsurge?" Labor Notes, March 22, 2023. labornotes.org.

Parenti, Michael. "The Wonderful Life and Strange Death of Walter Reuther." *CovertAction,* Fall 1995, 37–43.

4. Solidarity Takes Down the Whale

Blanc, Eric. *We Are the Union: How Worker-to-Worker Organizing is Revitalizing Labor and Winning Big.* Oakland: University of California Press, 2025.

Blatto, Anna. *A City Divided: a Brief History of Segregation in Buffalo.* Partnership for the Public Good (Partnership for the Public Good: April 2018). ppgbuffalo.org/files/documents/data-demographics-history.

Brown, Jenny. "Starbucks Workers Win Breakthrough Promise of Real Negotiations." Labor Notes, February 29, 2024.

Cohen, Lizabeth. *Making a New Deal: Industrial Workers in Chicago, 1919–1939.* Cambridge, England, New York: Cambridge University Press, 1990. Publisher description. www.loc.gov/catdir/description/cam024/89070810.html; Table of contents. www.loc.gov/catdir/toc/cam029/89070810.html.

"Current Starbucks Statistics." Union Election Data, 2024. unionelections .org/data/starbucks.

Hussain, Suhauna. "These L.A. Strippers Won a Union. But the Dance Isn't Over." *Los Angeles Times,* October 5, 2023.

Isidore, Chris. "Starbucks Workers at Buffalo Store Vote to Unionize." *CNN Business,* December 9, 2021. edition.cnn.com/2021/12/09/business /starbucks-union-vote/index.html.

Lanard, Noah. "Howard Schultz Came Out of Retirement to Destroy Starbucks' Union—and His Legacy." *Mother Jones,* 2023. www.motherjones.com /politics/2023/03/howard-schultz-starbucks-union-busting-buffalo-brooklyn.

Lichtenstein, Nelson, and Judith Stein. *A Fabulous Failure: the Clinton*

Presidency and the Transformation of American Capitalism. Princeton: Princeton University Press, 2023.

Marshall, Colin. "The First Starbucks Coffee Shop, Seattle—a History of Cities in 50 Buildings, Day 36." *The Guardian,* May 14, 2015.

Mathis-Lilley, Ben. "If Leaked List Is Accurate, Hillary's Cabinet Choices Would Have Enraged the Democratic Left." *Slate,* January 10, 2017. slate.com/news-and-politics/2017/01/hillary-cabinet-plans-leaked-sheryl-sandberg-at-treasury-starbucks-ceo-at-labor.html.

Pitkin, Daisy. *On the Line: a Story of Class, Solidarity, and Two Women's Epic Fight to Build a Union.* 1st ed. Chapel Hill, NC: Algonquin Books of Chapel Hill, 2022.

Press, Alex N. "Occupy Wall Street Made Me a Socialist." *Jacobin,* September 21, 2021. jacobin.com/2021/09/occupy-wall-street-anniversary-boston-dewey-square-99-percent.

Rudolph, Heather Wood. "Interview Insider: How to Get Hired at Starbucks." *Cosmopolitan,* September 11, 2014. www.cosmopolitan.com/career/interviews/a30807/interview-insider-starbucks-career-jobs.

Russell, Zachary A., Jack Fiorito, and Irene Padavic. "Union Beliefs and Activism: A Research Note." *Journal of Labor Research* 35 (2014): 346–57.

Scheiber, Noam. "Starbucks Falls Short After Pledging Better Labor Practices." *New York Times,* September 23, 2015.

Scott, Leonard C. Handwritten Notes on Counter-Union Campaigns, 1978; Scott, Leonard. Union-Prevention and Counter-Union Campaign Consulting Files #6474. Kheel Center for Labor-Management Documentation and Archives, Cornell University Library.

Smalls, Christian, and Jaz Brisack. "We're Organizing Unions at Amazon and Starbucks. We Won't Back Down." Ed. Daniel Denvir. *Jacobin,* 2022. jacobin.com/2022/05/amazon-starbucks-labor-union-busting-nlrb.

Swoboda, Frank. "Wal-Mart Ends Meat-Cutting Jobs." *Washington Post,* March 3, 2000.

Wellman, Judith. *Grass Roots Reform in the Burned-over District of Upstate New York: Religion, Abolitionism, and Democracy* (Studies in African American History and Culture). New York: Garland Publishing, 2000. Publisher description. www.loc.gov/catdir/enhancements/fy0652/00042948-d.html.

Winant, Gabriel. "A New Political Identity." *Dissent,* September 17, 2021. www.dissentmagazine.org/online_articles.

Winant, Gabriel. *The Next Shift: the Fall of Industry and the Rise of Health Care in Rust Belt America.* Cambridge, MA: Harvard University Press, 2021.

5. Organizing the Ivy League

Anderson, Stuart. "International Students Remain a Primary Source of U.S. Tech Talent." *Forbes,* August 19, 2021.

Bronfenbrenner, Kate. *Organizing to Win: New Research on Union Strategies.* Ithaca, NY: ILR Press, 1998.

Christensen, Chad. "The Employment of Part-Time Faculty at Community Colleges." *New Directions for Higher Education* 143, June 2008, 29–36.

National Labor Relations Board. "The Leland Stanford Junior University, 214 N.L.R.B. 621." Edited by National Labor Relations Board, 1974.

Robinson, Tilly R. "Embattled Harvard Professor John Comaroff Retires Without Emeritus Status." *Harvard Crimson,* August 2, 2024.

Roiphe, Katie. "Why Professors Should Never Have Affairs with Their Students." *Slate,* May 21, 2015.

Sainato, Michael. "Amazon Could Run Out of Workers in U.S. in Two Years, Internal Memo Suggests." *The Guardian,* June 22, 2022.

Young, Jeremy. "Christopher Rufo's Alarming and Deceptive Crusade Against Public Universities." *Time,* August 10, 2023.

Part III: New Strategies for a New World

McCartin, Joseph Anthony. *Collision Course: Ronald Reagan, the Air Traffic Controllers, and the Strike That Changed America.* New York: Oxford University Press, 2011.

6. The New Flints

Cooper, Ryan. "For Workers, Unions and Public Pressure Get the Goods." *American Prospect,* June 26, 2023. prospect.org/labor/2023-06-26 -workers-rail-unions-public-pressure/.

Domonoske, Camila. *Why Car Prices Are Still So High—and Why They Are Unlikely to Fall Anytime Soon.* National Public Radio, 2023.

Douglass, Ben, and Luigi Morris. "10 Reasons UPS Workers Are Voting 'No' on the Tentative Agreement." *Left Voice,* August 11, 2023. www.leftvoice .org.

Feliz Leon, Luis. "Inside the Teamsters' Historic Contract at UPS." *American Prospect,* July 25, 2023. prospect.org/labor.

Gordon, Aaron. "'The Worst and Most Egregious Attendance Policy' Is Pushing Railroad Workers to the Brink." *Vice,* April 5, 2022. www.vice.com/en /article.

Kamper, Dave. "'We're Workers, Not Robots.'" *Jacobin,* July 16, 2019. jacobin .com/2019/07/amazon-strike-prime-day-shakopee-fulfillment-center.

McCartin, Joseph Anthony. *Collision Course: Ronald Reagan, the Air Traffic Controllers, and the Strike That Changed America.* New York: Oxford University Press, 2011.

Moody, Kim. "Labor's New Terrain: Working on the Supply Chain Gang." *Labor Notes,* June 5, 2018. www.labornotes.org.

O'Donovan, Caroline, and Lauren Kaori Gurley. "Amazon Prime Day Causes Workplace Injuries, Senate Probe Finds." *Washington Post,* July 16, 2024. www.washingtonpost.com/business/2024/07/16 /bernie-sanders-amazon-investigation.

Press, Alex N. "Amazon Waged a Brutal Anti-Union Campaign. Unsurprisingly, They Won." *Jacobin,* April 9, 2021). jacobin.com/2021/04/amazon-bessemer-union-drive-vote-nlrb.

Rachleff, Peter J. *Hard-Pressed in the Heartland: the Hormel Strike and the Future of the Labor Movement.* 1st ed. Boston, MA: South End Press, 1993.

Samilton, Tracy. "Fiat Chrysler Will Plead to Criminal Charge in UAW Corruption Scandal." Michigan Public, January 28, 2021. www.michiganpublic.org/law.

Strategic Organizing Center. *In Denial: Amazon's Continuing Failure to Fix Its Injury Crisis.* April 2023. warehouseworkers.org/wp-content/uploads/2023/04/SOC_In-Denial_Amazon-Injury-Report-April-2023.pdf.

Vorse, Mary Heaton. *Labor's New Millions.* New York: Modern Age Books, 1938.

7. Somehow Striking Feels Good in a Place Like This

Avi-Yonah, Shera, and Andrea Salcedo. "Ronald Reagan Led an Actors Strike Decades Before His U.S. Presidency." *Washington Post,* July 14, 2023.

Blum, Ronald. "Minor Leaguers Form Union, 17 Days After Organizing Began." *AP News,* September 14, 2022. apnews.com/article/mlb-sports-baseball-major-league-players-association.

Goldstein, Luke. "Massachusetts Ballot Measure Criticized for Creating Gig Worker 'Company Unions.'" *American Prospect,* September 23, 2024. prospect.org/labor.

Littleton, Cynthia. "Revisting the 1980s SAG-AFTRA Strike with 'Mash' Stars, an Emmy Boycott and All-Night Negotiating Sessions: 'We're Going to Strike Like Hell.'" *Variety,* September 1, 2023. variety.com/2023/biz/news/sag-actors-strike-1980-similarities-differences.

Luff, Jennifer, and Sam Luebke. "Organizing: A Secret History." *Labor History* 44, no. 4 (2003): 421–32.

Maddaus, Gene. "SAG-AFTRA Candidates Urge Mediation: 'People Can't Afford This.'" *Variety,* September 7, 2023. variety.com/2023/biz/news.

McNary, Dave. "Protests Filed over SAG-AFTRA's Gabrielle Carteris Election Win." *Page Six,* September 4, 2019. pagesix.com/2019/09/04/protests-filed-over-sag-aftras-gabrielle-carteris-election-win.

Nolan, Hamilton. *The Hammer: Power, Inequality, and the Struggle for the Soul of Labor.* 1st ed. New York: Hachette Books, 2024.

Perlstein, Rick. *Reaganland: America's Right Turn 1976–1980.* New York: Simon & Schuster, 2020.

Press, Joy. "Meet the Writers Strike's Secret Weapon: Hollywood Teamster Boss Lindsay Dougherty." *Variety Fair,* May 17, 2023. www.vanityfair.com/hollywood.

Robb, David. "SAG-AFTRA Election Turns Ugly as Allegations and Threats of Lawsuits Fly Between Feuding Camps." *Deadline,* August 16, 2021. deadline.com.

Rodman, Howard A., and Alex O'Keefe. "With Their Five-Month Strike, Hollywood Writers Scored a Historic Victory." By Barry Eidlin. Jacobin, November 21, 2023. jacobin.com/2023.

Schor, Juliet B., and Veena Dubal. "Gig Workers Are Employees. Start Treating Them That Way." *New York Times,* January 18, 2021. www.nytimes.com/2021/01/18/opinion/proposition-22-california-biden.html.

Sharma, Shaan. "Unity: 2023 Letter to SAG-AFTRA LA Members." *Medium,* September 4, 2023. medium.com/@coalitionoflight.

8. It Doesn't Have to Be This Way

Brenner, Aaron, Robert Brenner, and Calvin Winslow. *Rebel Rank and File: Labor Militancy and Revolt from Below During the Long 1970s.* London, New York: Verso, 2010.

Brown, Keith Brower. "Auto Workers Escalate: Surprise Strike at Massive Kentucky Ford Truck Plant." Labor Notes, October 11, 2023. labornotes.org.

Fain, Shawn. "Exclusive: UAW President Shawn Fain on How the Auto Workers Won and What's Next." *In These Times,* November 7, 2023. inthesetimes.com/article/exclusive-interview-uaw-president-shawn-fain.

Feliz Leon, Luis, and Jane Slaughter. "Auto Workers Strike Plants at All Three of the Big 3." Labor Notes, September 15, 2023. labornotes.org.

Furman, Jonah. "Auto Workers to Vote on Direct Elections for Officers." Labor Notes, September 27, 2021. labornotes.org.

Juravich, Tom. "Beating Global Capital: A Framework and Method for Union Strategic Corporate Rsearch and Campaigns." In *Global Unions: Challenging Global Capital Through Cross-Border Campaigns.* Edited by Kate Bronfenbrenner. Ithaca, NY: Cornell University Press, 2007, 16–39.

Schwartz-Weinstein, Zach. "On Bill and Hillary Clinton's First Date in 1971, They Crossed a Picket Line." *In These Times,* February 9, 2016. inthesetimes.com/article/hillary-rodham-bill-clinton-and-the-1971-yale-strike.

"UAW's President Shawn Fain Makes Gains in Strike Talks, but Some Wonder: Has He Reached Too Far?" *CBS News Detroit,* October 23, 2023. www.cbsnews.com/detroit/news.

Index

Index

Index

Index

Index

About the Author

Currently a senior strategist at the Economic Policy Institute, **Dave Kamper** is an organizer and writer with twenty-five years of experience working for unions in Pennsylvania, Illinois, and Minnesota. Kamper has a PhD in history and his writing has appeared in *Jacobin,* Labor Notes, and other progressive publications. He lives in Minnesota.

Publishing in the Public Interest

Thank you for reading this book published by The New Press; we hope you enjoyed it. New Press books and authors play a crucial role in sparking conversations about the key political and social issues of our day.

We hope that you will stay in touch with us. Here are a few ways to keep up to date with our books, events, and the issues we cover:

- Sign up at www.thenewpress.com/subscribe to receive updates on New Press authors and issues and to be notified about local events
- www.facebook.com/newpressbooks
- www.x.com/thenewpress
- www.instagram.com/thenewpress

Please consider buying New Press books not only for yourself, but also for friends and family and to donate to schools, libraries, community centers, prison libraries, and other organizations involved with the issues our authors write about.

The New Press is a 501(c)(3) nonprofit organization; if you wish to support our work with a tax-deductible gift please visit www.thenewpress.org/donate or use the QR code below.